Decisions in Financial Management: Cases

Eugene F. Brigham
University of Florida

Timothy J. Nantell
University of Michigan

Robert T. Aubey
University of Wisconsin

Stephen L. Hawk
University of Wisconsin

Richard H. Pettway
University of Florida

Ernest A. Nagatta
University of Florida

HOLT, RINEHART AND WINSTON, INC.

New York   Chicago   San Francisco   Atlanta
Dallas   Toronto   Montreal   London   Sydney

Case 35 is an article entitled "Goodrich's Four-Ply
Defense" by Tom O'Hanlon, Associate Editor of *Fortune,* and
is reprinted by permission of *Fortune* magazine from its July 1969 issue.

Preface

Although corporation finance can be a fascinating subject, it is frequently difficult to arouse interest in the field on the part of many students. Feedback from students, especially nonmajors, suggests that many of them regard finance as either too mechanical or too theoretical. In an effort to overcome this attitude, we experimented with several different ideas. First, we learned from student questionnaires and discussions with students that their attitudes toward finance are closely related to our ability to relate the subject matter to the real world. If in our lecture on a particular topic we illustrate a point by reference to an actual situation, students' curiosity seems to intensify, their powers of concentration are sharpened, and we are able to impart more knowledge than if we dealt strictly with abstractions or hypothetical situations.

This recognition that we can improve the value of the course by increasing students' awareness of the relevance of finance led us to experiment with the case method. We tried various types of cases, ranging from the Harvard-type case to simpler, more structured ones, without notable success. The Harvard cases were too complicated for our introductory students —they spent an inordinate amount of time trying to figure out what steps they should follow to solve the case and what data were actually necessary and useful in reaching the solution. A number of the students were simply frustrated, although others, especially finance majors, were sufficiently interested in the cases to spend the perhaps excessive time required to learn something from them. On balance, we concluded that Harvard-type cases are not suitable for lower-level courses. We also experimented with a number of the simpler cases that are available in published form. Some of these are quite good, and our use of a few of them was successful. However, we found it difficult to use many of them because they were not designed to complement specific text assignments. This lack of direct relationship held even for the combined text-and-cases textbooks which some of us tried.

In informal discussions with our colleagues, the question was raised, Could we devise a set of cases that would retain the virtues of the Harvard-type cases—that is, motivate students by putting the text material into a real world context—while overcoming the drawbacks expressed above? Each of us had, over the years, collected a number of examples to use in our lectures as illustrations for the text material. Several of these examples had come from consulting experiences, some had been presented by corporate officers in executive development programs, and still others had been drawn from publications such as *Fortune*. We decided to restructure a limited number of these "case illustrations" into formal cases to see how useful they would be as teaching vehicles. As we proceeded, the following two rules were uppermost in our minds:

1. Each case should be keyed to a specific topic—ratio analysis, capital budgeting, dividend policy, and so on—in order to limit the scope of the case and thus make it correspond to a specific chapter of the textbook.
2. It should be possible for a student to work the case within a reasonable period of time. We used two hours as a target and tried to design the cases so that a student could, after having studied the relevant chapter, work the case in about two hours.

Our first experimental cases were used in both the undergraduate and graduate introductory finance courses, as well as in the second undergraduate corporation finance course. The cases were utilized somewhat differently in the various courses. More emphasis was put on student presentation in the graduate and, especially, the intermediate undergraduate courses, while in the introductory undergraduate course students were generally instructed to read the case and familiarize themselves with the situation, after which the instructor presented the solution to the case in class in lieu of a lecture on the text material. In spite of the fact that these early cases had many weaknesses, the instructors who used them received favorable evaluation reports from their students, and comments on the questionnaires indicated that this favorable reaction came about in large part *because of the cases*. On the basis of the success of the experiment, we decided to go ahead with the project and to write cases to complement each chapter in the major texts.

Although the initial cases had been highly successful, two problems were readily apparent. First, we concluded that it was virtually impossible to write a case that, on first use, would not have a number of ambiguities, omissions of essential data, or outright errors. This lead us to have each case worked thoroughly and independently by several teaching and research assistants before use in class. Even so, on every single case we made major modifications after using the case in class. Second, we found that the largest single problem with the initial cases had been that many students simply did not know how to begin to solve the case. We already had, of course, a written solution for each case, showing what decision the company had actually taken as well as the steps used in reaching the decision. Since we wanted the students to understand how the text material was used in reaching the decision, we simply added a series of questions at the end of each case to point in the direction of the decision process that was actually followed.[1] The inclusion of these carefully structured sets of questions greatly improved the usability of the cases; this was especially true at the introductory level.

We and others found that the cases make it much easier to motivate our students, majors and nonmajors alike. Students can now see the importance of finance in actual business decisions, and for many students this has transformed finance from a sterile, mechanical, "theoretical" subject into an interesting, pragmatic one. In addition, this has been accomplished without any loss of theoretical content. By showing the students why it is important to master theory, the cases actually *cause* them to learn more of the abstract, theoretical material than they would without the use of cases.

DIFFERENTIATION OF THIS CASEBOOK FROM OUR EARLIER BOOK

Our first casebook, *Cases in Managerial Finance,* published in 1970, met with more success than we had anticipated. However, as with all texts, and especially first editions, users of the book pointed out numerous errors and confusing sections and offered other suggestions for improvement. Some of these suggestions were obviously desirable, but we were less sure about others. In particular, we were unsure about how to handle suggestions that we expand the scope and depth of the cases. After all, we wanted to use the cases at the introductory level, or perhaps at the inter-

---

[1] While the questions point the student in the right direction, they certainly do not lead him by the hand to the correct solution.

mediate level for undergraduates, and too many extensions would lessen the book's usefulness for this purpose.

Our conclusion was that we really needed *two* books. Depending on the backgrounds and preparations of different groups of students, different textbooks are most appropriate, and the same thing holds true for casebooks. MBA students, or undergraduates who have relatively strong backgrounds in quantitative analysis, economics, and accounting can and should use somewhat more advanced instructional materials than less mature or well-prepared students. With this thought in mind, we designed *Decisions in Financial Management: Cases* for use in the more advanced introductory courses, or for intermediate level undergraduate courses.

More specifically, we think of our first book, *Cases in Managerial Finance,* as being most appropriate for use with the text *Essentials of Managerial Finance* and similar books, while the present casebook is most appropriate for use with *Managerial Finance, 4th Edition.* (In fact, the present set of cases were class-tested in classes which were also using the manuscript of the 4th edition of *Managerial Finance* as a text.)

We are grateful to a number of individuals for giving us suggestions which materially improved the book. Edward Altman, Steven Bolten, Santosh Choudbury, Irwin Harvey, Donald Knight, Charles Kroncke, Harry Magee, Robert Moore, John Morton, William Regan, Donald Sorenson, Milford Tysseland, J. Fred Weston, and William Weyers all made significant contributions. The Schools of Business at the Universities of Florida, Wisconsin, and Michigan provided us with intellectual support in writing and testing the manuscript. Finally, we must express our appreciation to the Holt, Rinehart and Winston staff, especially Jere Calmes, Rosalind Sackoff, and Sylvia Weber, for their support in bringing the book to completion.

The field of finance continues to experience significant changes and advances. It is stimulating to participate in these developments, and we sincerely hope that these cases will help to communicate the important issues in finance to future generations of students.

Gainesville, Florida
Madison, Wisconsin
Ann Arbor, Michigan
January 1972

E.F.B. / T.J.N. / R.T.A.
S.L.H. / R.H.P. / E.A.N.

Contents

Part I

Financial Analysis, Planning, and Control

Seafield Fashions

(Financial Analysis: Solution Given)

INTRODUCTORY NOTE

This first case differs from the others in the book in that a suggested answer to the case is provided. Our purpose in providing this solution is to give the student an idea of the type of analysis that was actually employed in the case itself at the time the decision was being made. Although the kind of analysis employed in the different cases throughout the book varies greatly depending on the type of material with which the case deals, this solution should provide a general idea of how one typically approaches the solution of a case.

STATEMENT OF THE CASE

Seafield Fashions, a small manufacturer of women's and girls' skirts and dresses, was organized by Neil Seafield in 1950. Seafield managed the firm until 1960, at which time he found that other business matters required most of his time. In March 1960, Edgar Dunlap, Executive Vice President of one of Seafield's competitors, was brought in as President and given complete responsibility for the operations of Seafield Fashions.

Since almost 60 percent of Seafield's sales are made during two busy seasons—just before Easter and in the early Fall—the company had been following a seasonal production schedule. One of Dunlap's first decisions was to change this practice so that Seafield produced at an even rate throughout the year. A second decision Dunlap made was to change Seafield's banking connections to Security National Bank. Primarily because Seafield frequently carried large cash balances, Security National had actively sought the account for two years prior to 1960. Although Dunlap agreed to move Seafield's account to Security National, he was able to reduce the size of Seafield's cash balances significantly without adversely affecting operations.

One result of these changes was that Dunlap found it necessary to borrow from Security National Bank prior to each of the big selling seasons. The loans were on a short-term basis, with the proceeds being used to increase finished-goods inventory in anticipation of heavy sales. The loans were made under a line of credit arrangement whereby the bank agreed to lend Seafield funds as they were needed up to a total of $110,000. The loan agreement stated, however, that total borrowing under the credit line must be retired after each selling season before Seafield started borrowing to build up inventory for the next selling season. Seafield had been taking full advantage of this line of credit, and until recently the company had been able to repay the loan in full before the next inventory buildup.

In late November 1968, Seafield began production for the 1969 Easter-Spring season. On December 18, Seafield used the first $30,000 of its line of credit to buy raw materials. By March 1, 1969, the company had borrowed a total of $108,000, and it was completing its spring production and making plans for the late summer season. Dunlap knew that if Seafield wanted to borrow again for the next inventory buildup, it would have to repay this $108,000. Before 1968, Seafield had been able to convert its inventory and accounts receivable into enough cash rapidly enough so that by March 31 the short-term loan was completely paid off. Since Seafield used a fiscal year that ended on March 31 rather than a calendar year, the bank loans did not normally appear on any of the company's annual financial statements. This, of course, made the company's ratios look better than would have been the case had the books been closed on December 31. However, in the years ending March 31, 1968, and March 31, 1969, Seafield was not able to repay the entire amount by March 31 (see Table 1.1).

Following the 1969 Easter season, Seafield found itself with a relatively large unsold finished-goods inventory. Because of this, the company was able to repay only $10,000 of the $108,000 loan by March 31. It was also having difficulty meeting its accounts payable obligations. Dunlap believed that these problems stemmed from the fact that, for the first time in Seafield's history, the company had failed to adjust rapidly enough to the new

Table 1.1

SEAFIELD COMPANY BALANCE SHEET
as of March 31[a]

	1967	1968	1969
Cash	$ 22,000	$ 14,000	$ 12,000
Accounts receivable	90,000	100,000	130,000
Inventory	105,000	180,000	300,000
Total current assets	$217,000	$294,000	$442,000
Land and building	24,000	40,000	70,000
Machinery	54,000	59,000	77,000
Other assets	1,500	800	100
Total assets	$296,500	$393,800	$589,100
Notes payable, bank	—	$ 39,000	$ 98,000
Accounts payable	$ 60,000	90,000	185,000
Accruals	18,000	22,300	31,600
Total current liabilities	$ 78,000	$151,300	$314,600
Mortgage	17,000	16,000	15,000
Common stock	75,000	75,000	75,000
Paid-in surplus	60,000	60,000	60,000
Retained earnings	66,500	91,500	124,500
Total liability and equity	$296,500	$393,800	$589,100

[a] Seafield follows an April 1 to March 31 fiscal year.

styles in women's dresses and, especially, skirt lengths. As a result, Seafield's Easter-Spring sales were significantly below previous levels for this season.

Dunlap decided that because sales in the next month and a half would not generate enough cash to repay the loan, some additional equity capital was needed. The Seafield family agreed to supply this capital, and Dunlap used part of the funds to repay the entire loan on May 5, 1969. Although the accounts payable balance remained higher than usual, it was reduced by $22,000.

In early May of every year, Dunlap renewed with the bank the $110,000 line of credit for the coming fiscal year. Renewal was usually automatic. On May 5, 1969, Dunlap made an appointment to see Bill Hudson, who has handled the Seafield account at Security since 1963. Dunlap was interested in increasing the credit line to $150,000, with the additional $40,000 to be used to reduce past-due accounts payable.

In the year since Dunlap last visited the bank, the Federal Reserve System, in an effort to slow inflation, had tightened credit conditions. In fact, on March 17, 1969, the prime rate rose to 7½ percent.[1] This tight money situation prompted Security National Bank to review critically all existing loans and to grant credit increases only on an exception basis.

Before the May 10 meeting, Hudson examined Seafield's operating statements for the last three years (see Tables 1.1 and 1.2). He noted that Seafield's profits had declined while total assets had increased. He also noted that Seafield had become a slow-paying account. Most of Seafield's suppliers offered a 2 percent cash discount on all bills paid within 10 days, but Seafield was unable to take advantage of this discount.

At the meeting with Hudson on May 10, 1969, Dunlap explained that Seafield had misjudged the market that spring and that the resulting sales decrease was the cause of the company's problems. He also mentioned that personnel changes had been made to insure that such misjudgments would not occur again.

Hudson told Dunlap that although this sales decline might be causing some of Seafield's working capital problems, he believed that the major problem was that Seafield was expanding its investment in assets too quickly. As Hudson saw it, the crisis following the spring season—the one that Dunlap had solved by increasing paid-in equity capital—was the inevitable result of too rapid an expansion over the last few years. The

Table   1.2

SEAFIELD COMPANY
INCOME STATEMENT, YEAR ENDED MARCH 31
(in thousands)

	1967	1968	1969
Net sales	$975	$1,013	$1,020
Cost of goods sold	794	815	824
Gross profit	$181	$ 198	$ 197
General and selling	75	80	83
Depreciation	8	9	13
Interest	8	8	9
Other	15	20	24
Income before taxes	$ 75	$ 81	$ 67
Taxes (50%)	38	41	34
Net income	$ 37	$ 40	$ 33

---

[1] The prime rate is the interest rate banks charge their best customers on short-term loans. The rate was subsequently increased to 8½ percent in the summer of 1969.

recent purchase of new equipment worth $25,000 and the purchase of one of the buildings which Seafield had been renting were given as two examples of actions that were creating an excessive cash drain on the firm. Hudson told Dunlap that, considering tight credit conditions and his feeling about Seafield's recent troubles, he would have to consider carefully both the $110,000 credit line and the request to increase the line by $40,000. He said that more analysis would be necessary and that he would inform Dunlap of Security National's final decision within the next two weeks.

Questions

1. Calculate the key financial ratios for Seafield Fashions and, based on these ratios, give a brief summary of Seafield's financial condition. Compare Seafield's ratios with those in Table 1.3.
2. What factors have caused the firm's declining liquidity?
3. What factors have caused the declining return on total assets?
4. What action should Hudson take concerning Seafield's request for a $150,000 line of unsecured credit?
5. Assuming the bank turned down the application to increase the credit line, what adjustments, if any, could you suggest that might make the new loan acceptable?

Solution: Answers to Questions

1.

	1967	1968	1969	Industry
Liquidity ratios				
Current ratio	2.78	1.94	1.40	1.80
Quick ratio	1.43	.75	.45	1.00
Leverage ratio—debt to total assets	32%	42%	56%	60%
Times interest earned	10.4	11.1	8.4	8.2
Activity ratios				
Fixed asset turnover	12.2	10.2	7.0	NA
Inventory turnover	9.27	5.65	3.40	9.00 times
Average collection period	33.2	35.3	46.0	29 days
Total assets turnover	3.30	2.58	1.74	2.60 times
Profitability ratios				
Profit margin on sales	3.8%	3.9%	3.2%	3.2%
Return on total assets	12.5%	10.2%	5.6%	8.3%
Return on net worth	18.4%	17.7%	12.7%	20%

Table   1.3

INDUSTRY RATIOS—AVERAGE, 1967–1969

Current ratio	1.8
Quick ratio	1.0
Inventory turnover[a]	9 times
Average collection period[a]	29 days
Total asset turnover[a]	2.6 times
Debt/total assets	60%
Times interest earned	8.2 times
Profit margin	3.2%
Return on investment	8.3%
Return on net worth	20%

[a] Based on year-end balance sheet figures.

The financial condition of Seafield is clearly deteriorating:
   a. Liquidity is poor and is getting worse. See Figure 1.1.
   b. Activity ratios reflect slow sales growth accompanied by large increases in current and fixed assets.
   c. Profitability has been falling. Return on net worth has been consistently low.
   d. The two leverage ratios that can be calculated show that Seafield is certainly not overburdened with debt. This accounts for the low return on net worth in relation to the other profitability ratios—return on net worth is below the industry average for all three years.
2. From Table 1.1 we see that current assets have expanded but that current liabilities have expanded more rapidly. Thus, Seafield's liquidity problem is basically a failure to keep current liabilities under control. To get the current ratio to the industry average of 1.8, Seafield would have had to sell $155,350 more out of inventory and use the resulting cash flow to pay off liabilities. Let X equal inventory reduction. Then

$$\frac{\text{Industry average}}{\text{current ratio}} = 1.8 = \frac{\$442,000 - X}{\$314,600 - X}$$
$$1.8\,(\$314,600 - X) = \$442,000 - X$$
$$X = \$155,350 = \text{inventory reduction}$$

Thus, if Seafield had not had such a disastrous Spring selling season, its liquidity would have been much improved.

3. Return on total assets $= \dfrac{\text{Profits}}{\text{Total Assets}}$

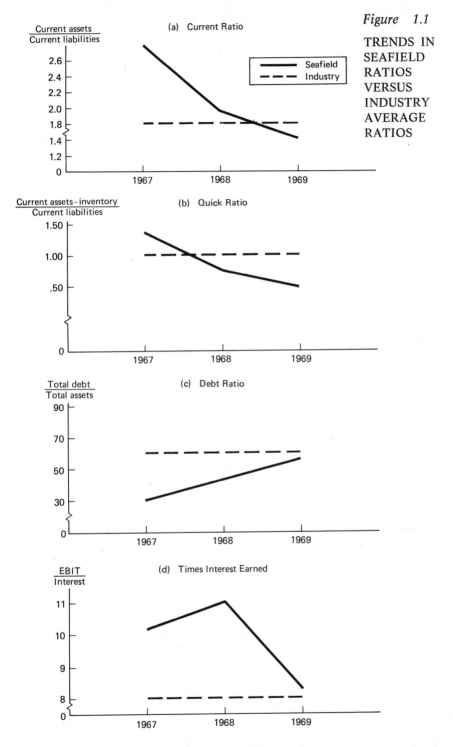

Figure 1.1

TRENDS IN
SEAFIELD
RATIOS
VERSUS
INDUSTRY
AVERAGE
RATIOS

9

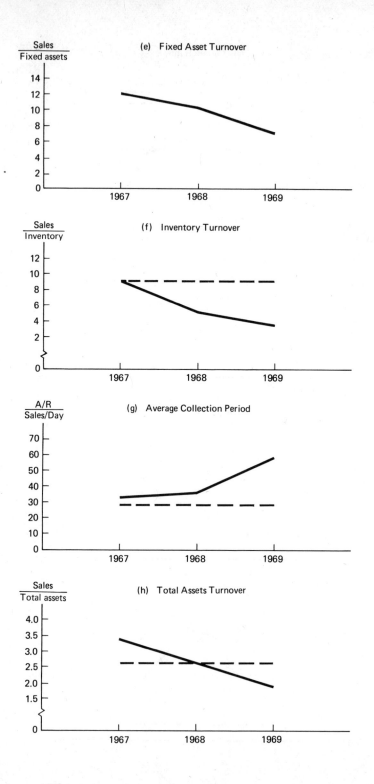

Sales / Fixed assets

(e) Fixed Asset Turnover

Sales / Inventory

(f) Inventory Turnover

A/R / Sales/Day

(g) Average Collection Period

Sales / Total assets

(h) Total Assets Turnover

10

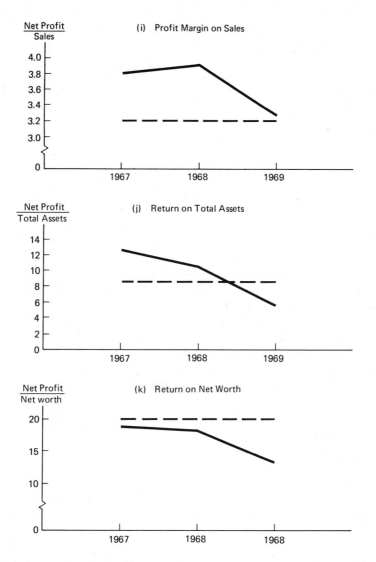

This ratio has been declining because total assets have been increasing faster than profit. This would tend to back up Hudson's position that asset growth (but *not* sales growth) has been too rapid.

A clearer picture of the causes behind the fall in return on total assets can be gained by defining that ratio as follows:

$$\frac{\text{Profits}}{\text{Total Assets}} = \frac{\text{Profit}}{\text{Sales}} \times \frac{\text{Sales}}{\text{Total Assets}}$$

$$= \text{Profit margin} \times \text{total asset turnover}$$

11

By examining these two ratios we can see that the decline in the return on total assets is caused by a decline in the asset turnover rate:

$$\text{Profit Margin} \times \text{Total Asset Turnover} = \frac{\text{Profits}}{\text{Assets}}$$

	Profit Margin	Total Asset Turnover	Profits/Assets
1967	3.8%	3.30	12.5%
1969	3.2%	1.74	5.6%

4. Seafield's ratios all indicate that its financial position is poor and deteriorating. Hudson was probably right when he said that only part of the troubles are directly related to the poor 1969 Easter season sales. Prior to this, the ratios had been falling, and this decline would probably have continued even in the absence of poor Easter sales. The bank must answer several questions:
    a. Will Seafield be able to repay the loan on schedule?
    b. If the loan cannot be repaid, can the bank recover its investment through bankruptcy proceedings?
    c. Is the company likely to carry substantial amounts of demand deposits?
    d. Does the bank have profitable alternative uses for its funds?
    e. Does the bank have an obligation to Seafield, and if so, would a failure to support Seafield at this time have unfavorable repercussions for the bank with its other customers?
        Hudson concluded that, all things considered, the $110,000 line of credit should not be renewed and, certainly, the $40,000 increase should not be granted, unless the loan was secured by some form of collateral. Hudson indicated that the bank would be willing to work out a security arrangement whereby inventories, accounts receivable, and unpledged fixed assets would be used as collateral for the loan. Alternatively, Hudson indicated that the bank would be willing to grant the increased credit if Neil Seafield, who has a sizable personal net worth, agreed to act as guarantor of the bank loan. Seafield was, in fact, willing to guarantee the loan, so the credit line was extended. In closing, we should note that Seafield Fashions engaged a management consulting firm to analyze the firm's operations and make recommendations for improving them. As a result of the controls recommended by the consultant, the company was able to solve its problems.

5. Typically, in a situation such as this, the bank would inform Seafield that the additional $40,000 line of credit would be granted only if the loan were secured in some manner—by a mortgage on fixed assets, a lien on the inventory, accounts receivable financing, or a guarantee by a third party. In this specific case, Neil Seafield agreed to guarantee the entire $150,000 line of credit, and on this basis the additional funds were made available.

Hartford Dairy, Inc.

(Financial Analysis)

Roger Elliot, Vice President and Loan Officer of the First National Bank of Hartford, was recently alerted to the deteriorating financial position of one of his clients, Hartford Dairy, Inc., by his bank's newly instituted computer loan-analysis program. The bank requires quarterly financial statements—balance sheets and income statements—from each of its major loan customers. This information is punched on cards and fed into the computer, which then calculates the key ratios for each customer, charts trends in these ratios, and compares the statistics on each company with the average ratios and trends of other firms in the same industry. If any ratio of any company is significantly poorer than the industry average, the computer output makes note of this fact. Also, if the terms of a loan require that certain ratios be maintained at specified minimum levels, and these minimums are not being met by a company, then the computer output notes the deficiency.

When an analysis was run on Hartford Dairy three months earlier, Elliot saw that certain of Hartford's ratios were showing downward trends and were dipping below the averages for the dairy products industry. Elliot sent a copy of the computer output, together with a note voicing his concern, to Eric Swenson, President of Hartford Dairy. Although Swenson acknowledged receipt of the material, he took no action to correct the situation.

While problems appeared to be developing in the financial analysis three months ago, no ratio was below the level specified in the loan agreement between the bank and Hartford Dairy. The latest analysis, however, showed that the current ratio was below the 2.0 times specified in the loan agreement. Legally, according to the loan agreement, the Hartford Bank could call upon the dairy for immediate payment of the entire bank loan, and, if payment was not forthcoming within 10 days, the bank could force Hartford Dairy into bankruptcy. Elliot had no intention of actually enforcing the contract to the full extent that he legally could, but he did intend to use the loan agreement provision to prompt Hartford Dairy to take some decisive action to improve its financial picture.

Hartford Dairy handles a full line of dairy products in northern Connecticut and the Hartford area. Seasonal working capital needs have been financed primarily by loans from the Hartford Bank, and the current line of credit permits the dairy to borrow up to $240,000. In accordance with standard banking practices, however, the loan agreement requires that the bank loan be repaid in full at some time during the year, in this case by February 1973.

A limitation on dairy products prices, coupled with a new labor contract which increased wages substantially, caused a decline in Hartford Dairy's profit margin and net income during the last half of 1971 as well as during most of 1972. Sales increased during both of these years, however, due to the dairy's aggressive marketing program.

When he received a copy of Elliot's latest computer analysis and Elliot's blunt statement that the bank would insist on immediate repayment of the entire loan unless the firm presented a program showing how the poor current financial picture could be improved, Swenson began trying to determine what could be done. He rapidly concluded that the present level of sales could not be continued without an *increase* in the bank loan from $240,000 to $340,000, since payments of $100,000 for construction of a plant addition would have to be made in January 1973. Even though the dairy has been a good customer of the Hartford Bank for over 50 years, Swenson was concerned whether the bank would continue to supply the present line of credit, let alone increase the loan outstanding. Swenson was especially troubled in view of the fact that the Federal Reserve recently tightened bank credit considerably, forcing the Hartford Bank to ration credit even to its best customers.

Questions

1. Calculate the key financial ratios for Hartford Dairy and plot trends in the firm's ratios against the industry averages. (See Tables 2.1, 2.2, and 2.3).
2. What strengths and weaknesses are revealed by the ratio analysis?

Table 2.1

HARTFORD DAIRY, INC.
BALANCE SHEET, DECEMBER 31

	1964	1970	1971	1972
Cash	$ 34,000	$ 51,000	$ 23,800	$ 17,000
Accounts receivable	136,000	204,000	231,200	323,000
Inventory	170,000	255,000	425,000	688,500
Total current assets	$340,000	$510,000	$680,000	$1,028,500
Land and building	51,000	40,800	108,800	102,000
Machinery	68,000	125,800	98,600	85,000
Other assets	40,800	23,800	6,800	5,100
Total assets	$499,800	$700,400	$894,200	$1,220,600
Notes payable, bank	—	—	85,000	238,000
Accounts and notes payable	74,800	81,600	129,200	255,000
Accruals	34,000	40,800	47,600	64,600
Total current liabilities	$108,800	$122,400	$261,800	$ 557,600
Mortgage	51,000	37,400	34,000	30,600
Common stock	170,000	170,000	170,000	170,000
Capital surplus	136,000	136,000	136,000	136,000
Earned surplus	34,000	234,600	292,400	326,400
Total liability and equity	$499,800	$700,400	$894,200	$1,220,600

Table 2.2

HARTFORD DAIRY, INC.
INCOME STATEMENT

	1970	1971	1972
Net sales	$2,210,000	$2,295,000	$2,380,000
Cost of goods sold	1,768,000	1,836,000	1,904,000
Gross operating profit	$ 442,000	$ 459,000	$ 476,000
General administration and selling	170,000	187,000	204,000
Depreciation	68,000	85,000	102,000
Miscellaneous	34,000	71,400	102,000
Net income before taxes	$ 170,000	$ 115,600	$ 68,000
Taxes (50%)	85,000	57,800	34,000
Net income	$ 85,000	$ 57,800	$ 34,000

3. What sources of *internal* funds would be available for the retirement of the loan? If the bank were to grant the additional credit and extend the increased loan from a due date of February 1, 1973

Table   2.3

HARTFORD DAIRY, INC.

	Dairy Products Industry Ratios (1972)[a]
Quick ratio	1.0
Current ratio	2.7
Inventory turnover[b]	7 times
Average collection period	32 days
Fixed asset turnover[b]	13.0 times
Total asset turnover[b]	2.6 times
Return on total assets	9%
Return on net worth	18%
Debt ratio	50%
Profit margin on sales	3.5%

[a] Industry average ratios have been constant for the past three years.
[b] Based on year-end balance sheet figures.

to June 30, 1973, would the company be able to retire the loan on June 30, 1973?*

4. Under what circumstances is the validity of comparative ratio analysis questionable?

5. In 1972, Hartford Dairy's return on equity was 5.38 percent versus 18 percent for the industry. Use the DuPont equation to pinpoint the factors causing Hartford to fall so far below the industry average.

6. On the basis of your financial analysis, do you believe that the bank should grant the additional loan and extend the entire line of credit to June 30, 1973?

7. If the credit extension is not made, what alternatives are open to Hartford Dairy?

---

*Hint: Funds available will come from profits and depreciation, as well as from a reduction of inventories and receivables if Hartford inventory turnover and average collection period are at industry average levels.

Nattell Corporation

(Breakeven Analysis)

After he received his M.A. in chemistry, with a specialty in plastics, Samuel Nattell was employed in the plastics division of a major chemical firm. His wife, Helen, managed the toy department of Lacy's, a large department store in Chicago, before their marriage in 1955. As a hobby, Mrs. Nattell designed, and Mr. Nattell produced, certain toy items, which they gave to their friends for Christmas, birthdays, and so on. These toys were very well received, and a number of the Nattells' friends asked to buy additional ones that they, in turn, could use as gifts. Also, Mrs. Nattell's successor in Lacy's toy department urged them to produce additional quantities to be marketed through the store.

In the summer of 1961, the Nattells decided to devote full time to the commercial production of toys, commencing January 1, 1962. Their initial plans were well laid: sales during the first year totaled $375,000, and they had grown to $3.9 million by 1972. The annual sales for each of the firm's first 11 years, together with certain other operating statistics, are presented in Table 3.1.

Total industry toy sales are generally quite stable, but, because of fads and fashions, individual firms experience considerably more instability than does the industry as a whole. Nattell, for example, "missed the market" in 1967 and 1970, when its new designs were not especially well received, and sales dropped significantly during each of those years.

Sales instability presents a problem for financial planning in the toy industry, and this problem is heightened by the seasonal nature of the

17

Table 3.1
NATTELL CORPORATION OPERATING DATA, 1962–1972 (in thousands)

	1962	1963	1964	1965	1966	1967	1968	1969	1970	1971	1972
Sales	$375	$471	$574	$720	$878	$750	$1,365	$1,800	$1,536	$2,900	$3,912
Less variable costs											
Cost of sales	288	362	447	549	667	592	1,024	1,350	1,167	2,291	3,051
Selling and administrative expenses[a]	19	24	29	36	44	38	68	90	79	145	196
Total variable costs	$307	$386	$476	$585	$711	$630	$1,092	$1,440	$1,244	$2,436	$3,247
	$ 68	$ 85	$ 98	$135	$167	$120	$ 273	$ 360	$ 292	$ 493	$ 665
Less fixed costs											
Rent							21	36	54	93	163
Depreciation	22	30	31	43	49	57	68	81	110	150	165
Interest	2	2	5	4	6	6	9	8	8	12	15
Taxes, property	3	5	4	7	6	7	12	23	33	45	67
Total fixed costs	$ 27	$ 37	$ 40	$ 54	$ 61	$ 70	$ 110	$ 148	$ 204	$ 300	$ 410
Earnings before taxes	$ 41	$ 48	$ 58	$ 81	$106	$ 50	$ 163	$ 212	$ 88	$ 193	$ 255
Less income taxes[b]	17	17	21	32	44	18	71	95	36	86	116
Profit after taxes	$ 24	$ 31	$ 37	$ 49	$ 62	$ 32	$ 92	$ 117	$ 52	$ 107	$ 139
Less dividends	10	10	10	10	10	10	10	10	10	10	10
Addition to retained earnings	$ 14	$ 21	$ 27	$ 39	$ 52	$ 22	$ 82	$ 107	$ 42	$ 97	$ 129
Net profits after taxes as a percentage of sales	6.4%	6.5%	6.4%	6.8%	7.1%	4.3%	6.7%	6.5%	3.4%	3.7%	3.6%

[a] Figured at 5 percent of sales.
[b] Taken as 22 percent on the first $25,000; 48 percent on the balance.

business. About 80 percent of all sales are made during the months of September and October, when stores are stocking up for the Christmas season. Collections are not generally made until January and February, when stores have received their Christmas receipts and are able to pay their obligations to the toy manufacturers.

Manufacturers have a choice of production techniques—they can either produce heavily during the April to September period in anticipation of the heavy fall sales, or they can follow a practice of level production during the year, storing output produced during the off-season period. The advantages of uniform production are that fixed asset requirements are reduced and better personnel can be obtained because of the full-time employment. The advantages of seasonal production, on the other hand, are that it reduces the danger of obsolescence due to style changes, decreases the storage problem, and reduces the need for financing to carry off-season inventories. Nattell has been following a seasonal production pattern, producing about 70 percent of its output during the April through September period and 30 percent during the remainder of the year.

Although the company has been continuously profitable, costs have been getting out of hand in recent years. The main plant was built in 1966, and additional capacity has been located in various rented buildings in the West Chicago area. The lack of centrally located production facilities and the need to train labor used during the peak production period are considered to be the primary reasons for the disproportionate increase in cost and the declining profit margin on sales. Sam Nattell is convinced that the firm should buy some land adjacent to the present plant, construct an automated, integrated production complex, and produce the year around. He also proposes to build a plant large enough to meet projected sales demand for some years into the future.

Helen Nattell, on the other hand, is worried about increasing fixed costs in a firm characterized by sales fluctuations. She believes that it would be sounder practice to slow down the firm's rate of expansion and consolidate its present position. To Helen, her husband's approach, although it would enable the firm to maintain its rapid growth and perhaps even make the family quite wealthy, would also jeopardize the continued existence of the firm.

It is estimated that variable costs will amount to approximately 85 percent of sales during 1973 if the present production setup is continued. Fixed costs for 1973 under the existing setup will be about $470,000 and $190,000 of this will be depreciation. If the expansion proposed by Sam Nattell—which calls for expenditures of approximately $5 million for plant, equipment, and increased working capital, all to be financed by a 10-year loan from an insurance company—is carried out, variable costs will fall to approximately 70 percent of sales. At the same time, fixed costs will rise to $1,175,000 a year. Depreciation in this case will be an estimated $600,000 a year.

Economies of expansion dictate that Nattell must take the step all at once if it is going to take it at all, since expansion by steps is too costly. If the expansion is not undertaken, Nattell believes that a larger profit margin can be restored by concentrating on cost control.

Since 1966, sales have been increasing at a 29 percent rate compounded annually. Nattell does not expect sales to continue to grow at this rate, but he does anticipate that a 20 percent annual sales increase can be attained over the next several years if the $5 million expansion is undertaken. The Nattells agree that without this expansion sales growth after 1972 will be about one half of the 20 percent projected if the expansion is completed.

Questions

1. (a) Calculate the breakeven point and (b) express it as a percentage of estimated 1973 sales, assuming present production methods are continued. (c) What is the estimated before-tax profit for 1973?

2. (a) Calculate the breakeven point and (b) express it as a percentage of estimated 1973 sales, assuming the proposed expansion is carried out. (c) What is the estimated before-tax profit for 1973, assuming a 20 percent sales growth?

3. Make a breakeven graph for Nattell showing both production methods.

4. At what level of sales would profits be equal under the two production methods?

5. What would happen to before-tax profit under each alternative if 1973 sales fell from the 1972 levels by about the same rate that sales fell in 1967 and 1970?

6. What are the cash breakeven sales levels for both production methods? (Assume that depreciation is the only non cash outlay.)

7. Estimate 1975 profits with and without the expansion. Assume that variable cost rates remain constant from 1973 to 1975.

8. (a) Assume that in 1973 sales are expected to increase by 10 percent over the 1972 level. What is the degree of operating leverage for this new level of sales if (1) the expansion is not carried out, and (2) the expansion is carried out? Use expected (that is, "formula") cost figures rather than actual income statement figures.

    (b) Using your answer to question 8.a, and additional information provided in the case, evaluate the relative risks and rewards associated with the alternatives of expansion and nonexpansion.

9. Do you think the Nattell Corporation should expand?

Case / 4

Plastics Unlimited, Inc.

(Financial Planning and Forecasting)

Plastics Unlimited was organized in 1958 to produce an assortment of molded plastic products for use in the furniture industry. Dallas Lillich, who received an M.A. in chemistry from the University of Wisconsin in 1956, had discovered a new type of hardened plastic material while a graduate student and had obtained a patent on the material. Noel Roberts, an engineer and close friend of Lillich, had worked with Lillich to uncover some special uses for the new material and to design molds that could be used in the production process. After designing and manufacturing several prototype parts for a major furniture firm, Lillich and Roberts obtained a purchase agreement for a large number of the parts from the furniture corporation.

On the basis of a patent on the chemical formula, the production plans, and the contract from the furniture company, Lillich and Roberts constructed a plan of operation for their proposed firm, Plastics Unlimited. With this operating plan they were able to secure the financial backing of Joe Crale, who had been in the real estate business in the Milwaukee area and had accumulated a sizable net worth. Crale's function in the new enterprise was simply to supply venture capital in return for a percentage of the operation. Plastics Unlimited was set up as a corporation, with Crale owning 40 percent of the stock, Roberts and Lillich each owning 26 percent, and Bob Webber, an accountant brought in to handle the controllership functions, 8 percent.

The new business was an immediate success. Production began in the summer of 1957 and the first sales were made in August. Sales for the five months in 1957 totaled only $38,000, but they jumped to $280,000 in 1958 and reached a total of $3.2 million by 1969. A large-scale physical expansion took place in 1969. Additional capacity was added at the Milwaukee home plant, and a small production facility was set up in Orlando, Florida. Until this time financing had been primarily from retained earnings, but the 1969 expansion was financed by a 15-year term loan, which was an addition to the long-term debt, from a major insurance company. The interest cost on the term loan was relatively high—8.75 percent—because of the high interest rates that prevailed during 1969. In addition, other terms of the loan were onerous. For example, the loan required Plastics to maintain a current ratio of 3 to 1 and forbade any additional long-term debt financing. The loan contract also contained a provision that called for the payment of an extremely severe penalty in the case of prepayment. Thus, if Plastics Unlimited wanted to repay the loan before its due date (for example, the firm might want to refinance its debt at lower interest rates), it would have to pay a certain sum in addition to the principal. Although the usual prepayment penalty amounts to one year's interest, Plastics Unlimited had been forced to agree to a provision calling for a sum equal to two years' interest.

Although the business had prospered, certain difficulties were developing among major stockholders. Roberts and Lillich, the President and Chairman of the Board, respectively, were dominating the affairs of the company, while Webber and Crale were cast in the role of dissenting minority stockholders. Specifically, Roberts and Lillich were both satisfied to receive large salaries from the company and did not want to distribute profits as dividends, while Crale and Webber would have preferred to distribute some of the profits as dividends. Further, Roberts and Lillich did not want to have the firm go public, because they disliked the idea of having to disclose financial information, while Crale and Webber both would have liked public ownership, largely to enable them to diversify their personal investment holdings. Finally, both Crale and Webber had objected to the insurance company term loan in 1969 because they felt that the prohibition on additional long-term debt financing, together with the current ratio requirement, would hamstring the firm in its future expansion plans.

Events during 1970 appeared to be bearing out Crale and Webber's position. The inflow of new orders exceeded projections, and the recently installed new plant facilities were already appearing inadequate. It was obvious that additional expansion would be required if the firm was to attain its full growth potential.

At the directors' meeting in September 1970, Crale and Webber made a joint presentation of their views on the company and its position. From a production and marketing standpoint, they said, the firm's policies had been excellent. However, from a financial standpoint management had been much less satisfactory. The major problems on the financial side, according to them, involved a failure to plan for growth and to arrange financing in an optimum manner. The two minority directors felt that the company would need additional equity capital—amounts in excess of what could be supplied by retained earnings—and that plans should be made for a public stock offering. This stock offering should be planned well in advance and should be coordinated with additional debt financing. They pointed out that the provisions in the term loan agreement, however, would make additional debt financing difficult, even though additional equity would be raised through the sale of stock and the company could take on additional debt without creating an imbalance in its financial structure. The two minority directors charged that these points should have been considered before finalizing the insurance term loan the previous year. This past mistake, they argued, made it even more important that a well-thought-out financial plan for the next few years be constructed at the present time.

For the purposes of such a plan, both Crale and Webber believed that the 1970 sales projection should be adjusted in light of the sales figure for the first eight months. Assuming that relatively as much business would be done in the last four months of 1970 as had been done in these months in 1968 and 1969, total sales for Plastics Unlimited for 1970 were projected at $3,700,000, with a 5 percent profit margin. Lillich and Roberts agreed that this was a realistic estimate. All four stockholders felt that a sales goal of $4,500,000 with a profit margin of 5 percent was reasonable for 1971.

Although the two majority stockholders admitted that some formal financial plan was necessary, they expressed the belief that any necessary expansion funds could come from retained earnings. Lillich indicated that this was possible because of the large increases expected in profits. The minority stockholders held that if Plastics Unlimited was to continue to grow, it would have to offer its stock publicly. All four stockholders agreed that high sales growth was their first objective, and therefore it was decided that the company should (1) make a projection of financing needs and (2) if outside funds were found to be necessary to support growth, make plans for obtaining these funds well in advance of the need for them.

Questions

1. Use the percent of sales method (using 1969 percentages) to forecast financial needs for 1970 and 1971 (see Tables 4.1 and 4.2).
2. What are the projected financial needs for 1970 and 1971 using the scatter diagram approach? (HINT: First make scatter diagrams

Table   4.1

PLASTICS UNLIMITED, INC.
BALANCE SHEET
(in thousands)

	1958	1963	1969
Cash	$ 11	$ 46	$ 105
Accounts receivable	89	367	820
Inventories	100	427	875
Current assets	$200	$ 840	$1,800
Net plant and equipment	105	460	1,085
Total assets	$305	$1,300	$2,885
Accounts payable	$ 55	$ 225	$ 550
Long-term debt	20	395	1,050
Capital stock	105	105	105
Capital surplus	100	100	100
Retained Earnings	25	475	1,080
Total liabilities and equity	$305	$1,300	$2,885

Table   4.2

PLASTICS UNLIMITED, INC.
INCOME STATEMENT
(in thousands)

	1958	1963	1969
Net sales	$280	$1,300	$3,200
Cost of goods sold	210	1,087	2,600
Gross margin	$ 70	$ 213	$ 600
Expenses[a]	55	122	434
Net income	$ 25	$ 91	$ 166

[a] Includes taxes.

of (a) total assets against sales; (b) current liabilities against sales;
and (c) current assets against sales. Then project these graphs to
1970 and 1971. Use the current assets projection to check for a
projected current ratio of less than 3 to 1.)
3. Are the assumptions involved in applying the percent of sales
method valid when forecasting financial needs for Plastics Unlimited for 1970 and 1971?
4. If enough funds cannot be generated through short-term debt and
retained earnings to meet the estimated requirements, what alternatives are open to the company?

California Canning Corporation

(Cash Budgeting)

When he returned from his coffee break at 10:30 A.M. on Monday, Ed Small, Assistant Treasurer of California Canning, found a note from Nat Taylor, Financial Vice President and Treasurer, asking him to come down to Taylor's office as soon as possible. When he arrived, Small found Taylor and Ed Young, Controller of the company, poring over a set of worksheet figures. Small quickly learned that because of the tight money situation that was developing in the spring of 1972, California Canning's bank was requesting all of its major loan customers to estimate loan requirements for the balance of the year.

Taylor had a luncheon appointment with Charles Marino, the bank loan officer who handled the California Canning Account, on the following Thursday—three days away. Taylor now wanted Young and Small to provide him with an estimate of financial requirements for the balance of the year. Taylor himself would be leaving on a business trip that same Monday afternoon and would not return until Thursday morning, just before the luncheon appointment. Young was tied up with the final preparation of the firm's federal income tax returns, so he would not be able to contribute much to the forecast. Accordingly, the primary responsibility for the estimate would fall on Ed Small.

At the Monday morning meeting, Taylor, Young, and Small agreed that what was needed was a cash budget. The firm had, of course, used cash budgets in the past, but one had not been prepared recently, and thus it was necessary to start from scratch. Just as the three men were beginning to discuss the mechanics of the actual cash budget preparation, Taylor's secretary came into the office with two messages: first, Taylor had just 45 minutes in which to drive to the airport to catch his plane, and, second, two CPAs were waiting for Young in his office—at $50 an hour each. A few minutes later Small was back at his desk, scratching his head and wondering how to begin the preparation of a cash budget.

Small first decided, on the basis of information already at hand, that no bank borrowing would be required before July; therefore, he decided to restrict his cash budget analysis to the period July 1 through December 31, 1972. Next, he obtained the following sales forecast from the marketing department:

May	$20,000
June	20,000
July	40,000
Aug.	60,000
Sept.	80,000
Oct.	40,000
Nov.	40,000
Dec.	10,000
Jan. 1973	20,000

He next obtained the following collection estimates from the credit and collection department: cash sales, 5 percent; collected the month following the sale, 80 percent; collected the second month following the sale, 15 percent.

Payments for labor and raw materials are typically made during the month following the month in which the costs were incurred. Total labor and raw materials costs are estimated for each month as follows (payments are made the following month):

May	$10,000
June	10,000
July	14,000
Aug.	98,000
Sept.	34,000
Oct.	26,000
Nov.	18,000
Dec.	10,000

General and administrative salaries will amount to approximately $3,000 per month; lease payments under long-term lease contracts will be $1,000 per month; depreciation charges are $4,000 per month; miscellaneous expenses will be $300 per month; income taxes of $7,000 will be due in September and December; and a progress payment of $20,000 on a new research lab must be paid in October. Small estimates that cash on hand on July 1 will amount to $15,000 and that a minimum cash balance of $10,000 should be maintained throughout the cash budget period.

Questions

1. Prepare a monthly cash budget for the last six months of 1972.
2. Prepare an estimate of required financing for each month during the period, that is, the amount of money that California Canning will need to borrow during each month.
3. Suppose receipts from sales came in uniformly during the month, that is, cash payments came in $\frac{1}{30}$ each day, but both purchase invoices and wages are paid on the fifth of the month. Would this have an effect on the cash budget—in other words, would the cash budget you have prepared be valid under these assumptions? If not, what could be done to make a valid estimation of financing requirements?

Case /6

Multiproducts, Inc.
(Financial Planning and Control)

Multiproducts, Inc. is a diversified multinational corporation that produces a wide variety of goods and services, including chemicals, soaps, toys, plastics, pollution control equipment, canned food, and computer software. The corporation's major divisions were brought together in the early 1960s under a decentralized form of management; each division was evaluated in terms of its profitability, efficiency, and return on investment. This type of organization persisted through most of the decade, during which Multiproducts experienced a high average growth rate in total assets, earnings, and stock prices.

Toward the end of 1970, however, these trends were reversed. The organization was faced with declining earnings, unstable stock prices, and a generally uncertain future. This situation persisted into 1971, but during that year a new president, Lynn Thompson, was appointed by the Board of Directors. Thompson, who had served for a time on the financial staff of I. E. du Pont, used the du Pont system to evaluate the various divisions. All showed definite weaknesses.

Thompson reported to the Board that a principal reason for the poor overall performance was a lack of control by central management over each individual division's activities. He was particularly disturbed by the consistently poor results of the corporation's budgeting procedures. Under that system, each division manager drew up a projected budget for the next quarter, along with estimated sales, revenue, and profit.

Then funds were allocated to the divisions, basically, in proportion to their budget requests. However, the estimates not only seldom matched the projections; they were usually off by a wide margin, either over or under the projected budget. These discrepancies, of course, resulted in a highly inefficient use of capital.

In an attempt to correct the situation, Thompson asked the firm's chief financial officer to draw up a plan to improve the budgeting, planning, and control processes. When the plan was submitted, its basic provisions included the following:

1. To improve the quality of the divisional budgets, the division managers should be informed that the continuance of wide variances between their projected and actual budgets would result in dismissal.
2. A system should be instituted under which funds would be allocated to divisions on the basis of their average return on investment (ROI) during the last four quarters. Since funds were short, divisions with high ROIs would get most of the available money.
3. Only about half of each division manager's present compensation should be received as salary; the rest should be in the form of a bonus related to the division's average ROI for the quarter.
4. Each division should submit all capital expenditure requests, production schedules, and price changes to the central office for approval. Thus, the company would be *re*centralized.

Questions

1. (a) Is it reasonable to expect the new procedures to improve the accuracy of budget forecasts?
   (b) Should all divisions be expected to maintain the same degree of accuracy?
   (c) In what other ways might the budgets be made?
2. (a) What problems would be associated with the use of the ROI criterion in allocating funds among the divisions?
   (b) What effect would the period used in computing ROI (that is, four quarters, one quarter, two years, and so on) have on the effectiveness of this method?
   (c) What problems might occur in evaluating the ROI in the crude rubber and auto tires divisions? Between the textile products and pollution control equipment divisions?
3. What problems would be associated with rewarding each manager on the basis of his division's ROI?
4. How well would Mr. Thompson's policy of recentralization work in a highly diversified corporation such as this, particularly in light of his three other proposals?

Part II

Long-term Investment Decisions

Case 17

Hooper Hydraulic Controls

(Replacement Decision)

Although he had been hired as a systems analyst after completing his M.B.A., Joel Cohen's first assignment at Hooper Hydraulic was in the finance area. When he reported to work for the first time, he was introduced to Miles Hooper, III, President of the company. Hooper had recently read an article in the *Harvard Business Review* dealing with the use of discounted cash flow methods versus the payback method in capital budgeting decisions. Hooper Hydraulic used the payback method in its own capital budgeting decisions, but after reading the article Hooper decided that his firm should begin to use one of the more sophisticated techniques. However, his concern at the time of his introduction to Cohen involved the use of the newer techniques in Hooper Hydraulic's sales presentations.

Hooper Hydraulic manufactures fluid control devices that have a wide variety of applications, including sanitation control systems, chemical and petroleum production, pipeline transportation, and hydroelectric power generation, among others. Although some of the control systems are specifically designed for individual customers, most are standard items that sell in the range of $25,000–$50,000. Since the control device is a specialized precision instrument, Hooper Hydraulic salesmen are primarily engineers or at least have some engineering background. The salesmen work with potential customers to show them the benefits of the Hooper

Hydraulic systems. Since most sales involve a number of separate systems, the total dollar volume that can be generated from a single order makes it well worthwhile for the salesmen to devote a considerable effort to closing each sale.

Hooper's marketing department has, up to now, emphasized only the engineering aspects of the products in promotional literature. Recently, however, the company has been giving increasing thought to emphasizing the economic aspects of the product line in its advertising campaigns. Also, management is considering giving the sales force a short course on the economics of replacement decisions in order to help them convince potential customers of the advantages of replacing old control systems with one of the new Hooper systems.

Hooper had just returned from a meeting with the marketing department on this matter when he met Joel Cohen. One of the points that had been brought up in the meeting was that Hooper Hydraulic, itself, used the payback method in its own internal budgeting decisions, and no one in the firm really understood the discounted cash flow techniques that had been described in the *Harvard Business Review* article. However, since the article indicated that use of the payback method frequently resulted in the decision not to make investments that would appear profitable under a discounted cash flow technique, Hooper believed that it was important to use one of the discounted cash flow techniques in promotional literature dealing with the economic aspects of the Hooper systems. In view of the very long service lives of most of Hooper Hydraulic's products, this avoidance of the payback method in sales discussions seemed particularly important.

When Hooper questioned Cohen, he was delighted to learn that Cohen had taken a finance minor in his M.B.A. program and was well versed in capital budgeting techniques. (Cohen, on his part, was surprised to learn that Hooper Hydraulic was still using the payback method.) In view of the urgency of the matter, Hooper asked Cohen to take an initial assignment working with the marketing department to develop promotional literature and to train the Hooper Hydraulic salesmen in the use of discounted cash flow capital budgeting techniques.

Cohen agreed to the assignment, and he and the Sales Manager, Charles Kane, decided to start by developing an analysis for one of the standard control devices—a unit that sells for $25,000 delivered. The following facts, which Kane indicated were fairly typical, were to be used in the illustrative material:

1. The equipment has a delivered cost of $25,000. An additional $2,000 is required to install the new machine; this amount is added to the cost of the machine for purposes of computing depreciation.

2. The new control device has a 20-year estimated service life. At the end of 20 years, the estimated salvage value is $1,000.
3. The existing control device has been in use for approximately 30 years, and it has been fully depreciated (that is, book value is zero). However, its value for scrap purposes is estimated to be $1,000.
4. The new equipment is to be depreciated on a straight-line basis. The applicable tax rate for the illustrative firm is 50 percent.
5. The new control device requires lower maintenance costs and frees personnel who would otherwise have to monitor the system. In addition, product wastage will be reduced. In total, it is estimated that the yearly savings will amount to $6,000 if the new control device is used.
6. The illustrative firm's cost of capital is 10 percent.

Questions

1. Develop a capital budgeting schedule that evaluates the relative merits of replacing the old machine with the new one. Use the net present value method.
2. Calculate the payback period (using after-tax cash flows) for the investment in the new control device.
3. Explain why the payback method puts long-term investments such as hydraulic control devices at a relative disadvantage vis-à-vis short-term investment projects.
4. Suppose one of the salesmen was making a presentation to a potential customer who used the internal rate of return method in evaluating capital projects. What is the internal rate of return on this project? (HINT: Be *sure* to use both present value of annuity table and present value of $1 table.)
5. What would be the effect on net present value if accelerated depreciation was used rather than straight-line depreciation? Give direction of change, not precise figures.
6. What would be the effect of an investment tax credit on the analysis? (An investment tax credit is a credit against income taxes equal to a specified percentage of the cost of an investment.)

Davis Trucking Company

(Capital Budgeting)

The Davis Trucking Company is a family operation owned by the three Davis brothers. Paul Woolcott, son-in-law of the oldest Davis brother, has recently taken over as assistant comptroller of the firm, with specific responsibilities for evaluating capital investment projects. Four major proposals are to be analyzed in detail. A brief description of each of these projects, together with its cost and the estimated cash flow (after tax profit plus depreciation) from each project over its estimated life, is presented in Table 8.1.

On the basis of *pro forma* cash flow statements for the coming year, Woolcott estimates that approximately $300,000 will be available from internally generated sources (depreciation and retained earnings) for capital investments. A 12 percent cost of capital for funds generated internally has been used in the past, and Woolcott sees no reason for departing from this figure. Any additional funds used for capital budgeting purposes will have to come from the three Davis brothers, and to make these funds available they will be required to liquidate security holdings. (The firm has a policy that Woolcott has been trying to change —so far unsuccessfully—of not using any debt capital other than a small amount of very short-term bank loans.) In discussions with the Davis brothers, Woolcott concludes that their opportunity cost on outside investments is 16 percent. In other words, funds over and above the

Table   8.1

CHARACTERISTICS OF INVESTMENT PROPOSALS

A. Expanded facilities at the Chicago terminal.
B. Alternative plan for the Chicago terminal expansion.
C. Purchase of four new tractor-trailer rigs.
D. Special handling equipment for a mining operation in Minnesota.

	A	B	C	D
Cost	$100,000	$100,000	$200,000	$100,000
Year 1	20,500	70,000	44,500	27,740
2	20,500	50,000	44,500	27,740
3	20,500	15,000	44,500	27,740
4	20,500	10,000	44,500	27,740
5	20,500		44,500	27,740
6	20,500		44,500	
7	20,500		44,500	
8	20,500		44,500	
9	20,500		44,500	
10	20,500		44,500	

NOTE: Returns include salvage value. No fractional projects can be undertaken.

$300,000 that will be generated internally are available, but the cost of any additional funds is 16 percent rather than the 12 percent cost of internal funds.

Woolcott is working on a five-year financial plan for the company, and he is developing estimates of capital investment opportunities and financial sources for this period. The plan at present is only in its formative stages, so Woolcott cannot formally incorporate it into his capital budgeting decisions for the present year. However, he is reasonably confident of two things. First, he thinks he will be able to persuade the Davis brothers to use debt financing and that this will lower the firm's cost of capital. Second, he feels that a recently installed employee incentive program designed to generate new investment ideas will bear fruit, with the result that the firm will, in the future, have better investment proposals available to it—that is, Davis Trucking will be able to invest more money, at higher rates of return, in the future than it has been able to in the past.

Questions

1. Calculate (a) the internal rate of return (IRR) for each project and (b) the net present value (NPV) using both 12 and 16 percent. (HINT: For project B's IRR, try 24 percent.)

2. What projects should the Davis Trucking Company take on during the coming year?

3. (a) Projects A and B are mutually exclusive. Draw a graph of NPV versus discount rate for A and B using, in part, your answers to 1 (a) and 1 (b).

   (b) Which project is superior?

   (c) If the firm had previously introduced debt into its capital structure so that its overall cost of capital were now 10 percent, how would this affect your answer to (b)?

4. Given that the return on project A is representative of investment opportunities generally found in the trucking industry, would it be reasonable for Woolcott to claim that project B will generate a return of approximately 24 percent over its four-year life?

5. If Woolcott is confident that he will be able to generate more and better projects next year and in the years to come, but is relatively doubtful that he will be able to persuade the Davis brothers to employ debt financing, how might this influence his recommendations? Could there ever be a situation in which project D would be advisable?

Townes Computing Corporation

(Capital Budgeting: Uncertainty)

Warren Rose is about to make his first major decision as president and chief executive officer of Townes Computing Corporation, a business organized in 1966 as a computer software and leasing firm by three former International Business Machines employees. The fledgling company's record of growth and profitability was extraordinary during the period 1966 through 1969, with earnings amounting to over $700,000 in the third year of operation. Because investors assumed that this earnings trend would continue, the company's stock sold at approximately 200 times earnings during 1969, giving the firm a total market value of $140 million. At this point, each of the three founders of the company held about 10 percent of the stock, giving each of them a paper net worth of approximately $14 million on an investment of about $40,000; the remaining 70 percent of the stock was owned by public stockholders, principally mutual funds.

The extraordinary expansion during the first three years of the new company's life was financed partly by the sale of the stock now owned by the public and partly by bank credit. The bank credit consisted, for the most part, of short-term loans used to finance equipment that the company purchased and then leased to clients. Each client generally leased a package consisting of (1) computer hardware and (2) programs especially designed and written by Townes' programmers to meet the special needs of the client company.

The original founders made two mistakes. First, they put up their own stock in the company as collateral for a personal bank loan, using the proceeds of the loan to buy the stock of other computer companies. Second, Townes Computing purchased a large quantity of third-generation computer hardware just before the announcement that a major computer manufacturing company was releasing a fourth-generation computer that would make Townes' newly acquired equipment obsolete. After this announcement, Townes was forced to lease its old equipment at much lower rates than had been anticipated, and, at the same time, it was required to revamp, at considerable cost, a number of its older computer programs. The net result was that profits skidded from $700,000 in 1969 to $23,000 in 1970 and, further, to a loss of $2,240,000 in 1971.

This sharp earnings decline drove the price of the stock down from its high of $123 to $6 a share. The fall in the price of the stock reduced the value of the stock that the three partners had put up as collateral for their personal bank loan. When the market value of the securities dropped below the amount of the loan, the bank, acting under a clause in the loan contract, sold the pledged securities on the open market to generate funds to repay the bank loan. This very large sale of stock further depressed the price of Townes Computing's stock, so the proceeds from the stock sale were not sufficient to retire the bank loan. The bank then sued the three founders of Townes Computing for the deficit and won a judgment which required them to turn over their other stocks to the bank. This additional stock was not sufficient to pay off the loan in full, and the final result was bankruptcy for the three men. Thus, in just three years, each of the founders of Townes Computing saw their net worth go from $40,000 to $14 million to zero.

The corporation itself was badly damaged by this series of events, but it remained intact. When the three major stockholders lost their shares in the company, the largest institutional investors, who now had control of the firm, decided to put in a completely new board of directors and to install Warren Rose as president and chief executive officer. The institutions would have preferred to sell their holdings of the stock, but they recognized that if they attempted to do so they would further depress the market—in other words, they were "locked in."

Rose was given significant stock options in the company and was told that he was expected to restore the firm's lost luster. There was some debate among the institutional stockholders concerning the firm's underlying philosophy; the more aggressive institutions wanted to see the company operated aggressively, while the conservative holders preferred a more cautious approach. The issue was never resolved, and Rose concluded that he could decide the risk posture of the firm for himself.

Rose was certain that his own position would be on solid ground if he followed a high-risk, high-return policy—and was successful. His stock options under these conditions would be extremely valuable, and his salary would be assured. However, he would be out of a job if he followed such a policy and the company was not successful. On the other hand, he was not altogether sure what his position would be if he followed a conservative policy—the company could survive and make a modest profit, but he might still eventually lose his job.

The first major decision Rose must make deals with a system for transmitting data from clients, storing the data, and retrieving it for later processing. Three alternative methods for the transmission stage are available; some information on these methods is presented in Table 9.1. Under alternative A, U.S. Telephone & Telegraph Company will, at a cost of $1,250,000, provide all necessary receiving and storage equipment, and transmission lines, to Townes Computing. The actual cash flows from this

Table 9.1

TOWNES COMPUTING CORPORATION
ALTERNATIVE METHODS FOR TRANSMISSION STAGE

Inflows

	Project A		Project B		Project C
Probability	*Cash Inflows*	*Probability*	*Cash Inflows*	*Probability*	*Cash Inflows*
.01	$ 50,000	.05	$ 50,000	.05	($2,750,000)
.05	100,000	.10	100,000	.10	0
.44	150,000	.35	150,000	.35	250,000
.44	200,000	.35	200,000	.35	500,000
.05	250,000	.10	250,000	.10	750,000
.01	300,000	.05	300,000	.05	1,000,000

Outflows (cost)

	Project A		Project B		Project C
Probability	*Cash Outflows*	*Probability*	*Cash Outflows*	*Probability*	*Cash Outflows*
1.0	$1,250,000	.05	$ 900,000	.05	$ 500,000
		.15	950,000	.15	800,000
		.60	1,000,000	.60	1,000,000
		.15	1,050,000	.15	1,200,000
		.05	1,100,000	.05	1,500,000

system would depend partly on sales of the new service and also on the level of operating cost incurred by Townes. Alternative B calls for Townes to assemble its own storage and retrieving equipment, but to lease transmission lines from U.S. Telephone & Telegraph. Initial costs under this system are not known with certainty. Alternative C calls for the installation of a new microwave data transmission process that is totally untested. Installation costs are highly uncertain, as are cash flows from the service if it is successfully installed.

Rose noted that if the worst possible cash inflows resulted for investment C, then Townes would be insolvent and would be forced to declare bankruptcy. All of the cash outflows will be incurred in the first year. He estimates that the actual first-year cash flow from each project, whatever the flow turns out to be, will continue for the entire 10-year life of each project. Of course, if the large first-year loss on project C is incurred, the service will be dropped because the company will be bankrupt.

Questions

1. Calculate the expected value of the cash flows from each project.
2. Find the expected internal rate of return on each project.
3. Find the net present value of each project using a 12 percent cost of capital. Could the net present value and internal rate of return result in decisions that conflict with the cash flow patterns given in the case?
4. Is it reasonable to use a 12 percent cost of capital for each project even though their costs and return probability distributions differ? What methods for dealing with risk are available to Mr. Rose?
5. Calculate the standard deviation of the expected inflows for Project A. For Projects B and C the standard deviations are $45,950 and $731,000. Use these figures to develop measures of the relative riskiness of the three projects.
6. In reaching a decision on the projects, whose viewpoint should be taken—Rose's, that of the aggressive investors, or that of the conservative investors—and how does this affect the solution?
7. Which of the projects, if any, do you think Rose should accept?
8. If the returns from Projects A, B, and C had had strong negative correlation with the normal expected earnings of the firm, would this affect your estimates of expected value? Would you still consider C to be the riskiest project? How would it affect the overall riskiness of the firm? The overall cost of capital?
9. As an extension of the case assume that you are comparing Project A's inflows with a fourth project having a certain $1,250,000 cost and expected to yield the following returns:

Project D

Probability	Cash Inflow
.3	140,550
.6	175,000
.1	278,350

Compute the expected return and standard deviation for Project D. Which project is more risky, A or D? What problems arise in interpreting the standard deviation of a probability distribution such as that of Project D?

Worldwide Minerals, Inc.

(Capital Budgeting: Uncertainty)

Lawrence Wright, Vice President, Finance, is preparing his report for the monthly directors' meeting of Worldwide Minerals. A number of important issues are on the agenda, and Wright himself has not completely formulated opinions on several of the topics.

The first issue involves what some of the directors call the "foreign aid project." The government of Monrovia, one of the new West African nations, has agreed to give Worldwide some important offshore oil concessions—provided Worldwide agrees to take on one of the four investment projects listed in Table 10.1. Project A involves the development of a rubber plantation which will produce no income for 10 years, but which will be worth approximately $440 million at the end of the 10th year. Project B involves the construction of a hydroelectric dam and power station; revenues from this project are expected to amount to $20 million a year. Project C calls for the construction and operation of a railroad facility, whose revenues should increase as Monrovia's economic development progresses. Project D involves the development of a strip mining operation in the central highlands; its revenues will be highest in the first year, and the mine will be completely exploited after four years.

The projects have all been examined by the World Bank, an organization that finances economic development, largely with the support of the U.S. government. The bank's estimates of the cash flows for each of the

Table 10.1

WORLDWIDE MINERALS, INC.
FOUR ALTERNATIVE INVESTMENT PROJECTS

	Rubber Plantation A	Power Station B	Railroad C	Mining Operation D
Cost of Project	$75,000,000	$96,500,000	$100,000,000	$95,000,000
Returns in Years				
1	$ 0	$20,000,000	$11,600,000	$58,000,000
2	0	20,000,000	13,500,000	40,400,000
3	0	20,000,000	15,600,000	15,600,000
4	0	20,000,000	18,000,000	9,100,000
5	0	20,000,000	21,000,000	0
6	0	20,000,000	24,400,000	0
7	0	20,000,000	28,300,000	0
8	0	20,000,000	32,800,000	0
9	0	20,000,000	38,000,000	0
10	463,000,000	20,000,000	44,100,000	0

projects are given in Table 10.1. The bank considered all four projects to be economically feasible; its economists were aware of the potential oil resources when they made the study. Although the projects admittedly carry a high risk (the cash flows in each year for each project are equally risky, although the cash flows for *different* years are *not* equally risky), the World Bank would be willing to finance the four projects. However, the bank's funds are insufficient to allow it to lend the Monrovian government the funds necessary to complete more than three of the four projects. The Monrovian government has, therefore, decided to tie the granting of the oil concession to the investment in one or more of the listed projects.

Some of the directors of Worldwide Minerals consider the projects to be "foreign aid"; they think that the costs are likely to be underestimated and the returns overestimated, with the result that Worldwide will lose heavily on any project it assumes. Other directors, on the other hand, are impressed with the research done by the World Bank economists. The bank's report on the projects hinted that costs are very conservatively estimated, while revenues may well run double those shown in the table.

Wright concludes, first, that the projects all carry considerable risk and, second, that no one of them is obviously better than any other. His personal preference is not to undertake any of the projects and, therefore, not to be granted the oil concession. A majority of the board members have, however, indicated that they favor taking on one of the projects in order to obtain the concession. Several board members have even suggested that all of the projects look interesting, and, given Worldwide's large cash flows and unused borrowing capacity, these directors will probably suggest that Worldwide take on more than one of the projects. A spokesman for this group recently sent Wright a memorandum indicating that, according to his rough estimates, each of the listed projects has a rate of return in excess of the 10 percent cutoff point Worldwide Minerals uses in capital budgeting. He also pointed out that if Worldwide does not undertake the Monrovian venture, it will probably have to increase cash dividends to get rid of its cash flows from operations.

Another topic that is likely to be brought up at the forthcoming directors' meeting is the cutoff rate of return itself. Worldwide Minerals has been using 10 percent as the cutoff point, or "hurdle rate," for all projects. This procedure has been criticized in the past by some directors on the grounds that less risky projects should be subject to a lower cutoff point, while higher-risk projects should have to pass a higher hurdle rate. Justin Dark, president of a major bank and a long-term Worldwide Minerals board member, has long advocated the use of differential rates for different risk projects, and he recently sent Wright the figures shown in Table 10.2. These figures, according to Dark, support his contention

Table 10.2

COST OF CAPITAL ESTIMATES FOR U.S. FIRMS WITH DIFFERENT DEGREES OF RISK[a]

Justice Department Studies	
Large public utilities	8%
Grocery chains	9%
Major chemical producers	10%
U.S. computer corporations	10%
International oil companies	11%
Smaller computer companies	15%
Small oil drilling and exploration companies	20%
Public Utility Rate Case[b]	
Short-term government bonds	6%
Long-term government bonds	6½%
Long-term electric utility bonds	7½%
Electric utility stocks	11%
(electric utilities: average of bonds and stocks)	8½%
Industrial stocks: major firms	12%
(industrials: average of bonds and stocks)	10%
Small industrial company stocks	17%

[a] Figures developed as a table in a recent antitrust case.

[b] Figures presented in a recent case before a utility commission seeking to determine a proper rate of return for a large electric utility company. It should *not* be assumed that a U.S. utility company and a Monrovian utility carry the same degree of risk.

that projects with differing degrees of risk should be capitalized at different rates. Wright believes that although the four projects are not equally risky, they are at least as risky as the riskiest companies on Dark's list.

One final bit of information that Wright is pondering as he thinks of his report came in a telephone call he just received from Marshall DeRossett, President of Worldwide Minerals. DeRossett suggested that, assuming Worldwide Minerals goes ahead and takes on one of the projects in order to obtain the oil concessions, the project should be either *B*, the hydroelectric power station, or *C*, the railroad installation. His argument is that these two projects tie in quite well with the oil concession because, if the oil drilling turns out to be successful, the economy of Monrovia would boom. In this event, both the power station and the railroad should be highly prosperous. Thus, Worldwide's earnings would be improved substantially by a major strike in the oil drilling operations—earnings would flow in from the oil itself, and the resultant economic boom would cause the power station or railroad investment to turn out better than anticipated. These higher earnings would naturally be reflected in the price of Worldwide's common stock.

Worldwide Minerals has already spent $15 million on geologic surveys for the offshore oil concession. These expenditures include seismographic work and the drilling of one exploratory well. Seismographic data indicate a high probability of a sizable oil strike, and the one well that was drilled did produce a substantial flow of oil. Assuming Worldwide goes ahead with the project, it must spend an additional $20 million on exploratory wells to determine the size of the oil field. This drilling will take about one year to complete. Depending upon the size of the field, the project may or may not be commercially feasible. It is estimated that the chances are 80 percent that the exploratory drilling will lead to the conclusion that the field is commercially profitable. There is a 20 percent probability that the additional drilling will indicate that the field cannot be developed commercially and that Worldwide should not go on with the project. Assuming the field can be developed, an additional $50 million must be spent to provide storage facilities, transportation facilities, and development wells. If the firm goes on with the project, expected returns are as follows:

Probability	Annual Returns (in millions)
.10	$ 2
.20	10
.40	20
.20	30
.10	50

Worldwide is not sure how long the annual returns will continue, but probability estimates are as follows:

Probability	Life of the Project (in years)
.15	5
.20	15
.30	25
.20	35
.15	45

In spite of the obvious uncertainties in the offshore venture, Worldwide officials feel that this project is about as risky as the average project taken on by the company.

Worldwide must commit itself to a "foreign aid" project before it goes ahead on the additional exploratory wells; that is, it cannot wait until the results of the additional exploratory drilling are available before deciding on the special government project. If the company is to continue with the offshore oil concession project, it must commit itself to at least one of the four projects at this time.

Questions

Wright proposes to deal with the following questions in his report to the board of directors:

1. How does the information in Table 10.2 bear on the choice among the four projects listed in Table 10.1?
2. What is the *expected* rate of return on the *remainder* of the expenditures for the offshore oil project? Should the $15 million of sunk costs be disregarded, or how should these costs be taken into account? (NOTE: Assume all outlays are made immediately and inflows begin in one year.)
3. Assuming Worldwide goes ahead with one of the four projects, but only one project, which one should it choose? Use the internal rate of return method (and try 16 percent for projects C and D), but be sure to consider risk differentials. In terms of the timing of cash flows for project A, are there any additional characteristics which should be considered other than the expected present value and internal rate of return of the investment?
4. Should Worldwide Minerals actually take on more than one of the projects?
5. What additional information would be useful in making the present decision? What is the feasibility of obtaining such information, and how, specifically, would it be used if it was available?

Part III

Financial Structure and the Cost of Capital

Crimmins Equipment Company

(Financial Leverage)

The Crimmins Equipment Company, a specialty manufacturer of sporting goods, was founded in 1952 by William Crimmins, a former star athlete at Southeastern University. From the beginning, Crimmins Equipment capitalized on the name and reputation of its founder, but, in addition, the company also produced top-grade equipment and pioneered the development of a number of new types of equipment, such as football kicking tees and fiberglass vaulting poles. Crimmins and his staff maintained contacts with many coaches, players, and others associated with various amateur and professional sports, and through these contacts the company received many ideas for new products, as well as help in the development of these products. Typically, an individual who conceives an idea for a new type of equipment works with Crimmins Equipment under a contract calling for the individual to help with the development of the items and to receive royalties based on the number of units sold.

In late 1972, Crimmins Equipment engineers finished the final designs and production plans for a new and revolutionary type of exercise machine, the Autoexerciser. The concept of the Autoexerciser was developed by the trainer of a major professional football team, and preliminary studies of the machine suggest that it will also be adopted for use by most other professional football teams as well as professional baseball and basketball teams. The Autoexerciser, which will retail for about $200, is also suitable for home use, and Crimmins is hopeful of developing a large volume of sales to individuals. Just how receptive the market will be for the new machine is, however, highly uncertain; the sporting goods field is highly competitive and heavily dependent on advertising, and it is difficult to predict the success of a new product.

Adding to the uncertainty associated with the project is the fact that production costs have not yet been determined with any degree of accuracy. Crimmins' production people think that the Autoexerciser can be produced at a cost of approximately $150 per unit, and if this cost estimate is met, the company will net $30 per unit after a $20 selling cost, assuming a sales price of $200. However, the production manager has warned that the actual production cost could run as high as $250, in which case the retail price of the machine would have to be approximately $300 per unit. The market for equipment of this type has a relatively high degree of price elasticity, so the sales volume would be reduced markedly if the price were set as high as $300.

In spite of these uncertainties, preliminary estimates, including market forecasts and engineering cost studies, convinced Crimmins and the remainder of his management team that the company should go ahead with full-scale production of the Autoexerciser. Further, management has decided that since an expansion is necessary for its production, the firm should also make additional plant expansions to meet normal growth requirements in other product lines. The capital outlays and additional working capital needs require a 40 percent increase in total assets during 1973.[1]

To finance this expansion, Crimmins Equipment has the alternative of using 8 percent bonds or new common stock that can be sold at a price to yield the company $25 per share. William Crimmins, Chairman of the Board and major stockholder in the company, will have to make the final decision concerning whether to use stock or bonds. In a recent directors' meeting, two positions were presented, and Crimmins is now trying to decide the relative merits of each one.

First, Frank Scott, a director and chairman of the board of Scott & Company, the investment banking house that has handled Crimmins Equipment's long-term financing needs, recommends strongly that the company choose debt financing at this time. Scott believes that inflation is likely to be persistent in the U.S. economy and that "debt incurred now can be repaid in future years with cheap dollars." Scott also indicates

---

[1] Some of the requirements for funds could be met by retained earnings, but disregard this factor; that is, assume the 40 percent increase must be met entirely from outside funds.

that his discussions with stockholders of the company—and Scott's firm has many customers who own Crimmins Equipment stock—indicate that the investing public is, at the present, more interested in companies whose securities are highly leveraged than in conservative firms; that is, investors are, according to Scott, risk-takers.

Garrett Fitzgibbons, Vice President, Finance, takes the opposite point of view. Fitzgibbons argues that the firm's risk will be increased considerably if it sells additional debt at this time. According to Fitzgibbons, the sales forecasts are favorable, but if costs of the new machine are higher than anticipated, or if sales fall below the anticipated level, the company could be in serious difficulty. Fitzgibbons also notes that the company's commercial bankers have expressed their concern over seeing the debt ratio rise above its present level.[2] Finally, Fitzgibbons stresses, if the company uses additional common stock now, its financial position will be strong, and should demand exceed expectations and new facilities be required in the near future, the company would be in an excellent position to sell debt at a later date. Although it is not in his report, Crimmins also recalls that Fitzgibbons has expressed a belief that interest rates are high at the present time and that if the company defers debt financing, it may be able to obtain debt at a lower cost in the near future.

The currently outstanding debt carries a 6 percent interest rate. Because the general level of interest rates is higher now than when the old debt was issued, the new debt would carry an 8 percent cost. There is, however, a provision in the contract on the presently outstanding debt which states that it must be retired (without penalty) before new long-term debt is issued if the new debt has a higher interest rate. Scott indicated to Crimmins that this provision would present no problem; the company would be able to sell enough new debt ($3 million) to provide funds both for the expansion and to pay off the old debt.

When Crimmins pressed Scott and Fitzgibbons for information on the effect of increasing the debt ratio on the price-earnings ratio, there was some disagreement. Fitzgibbons felt that the current price-earnings ratio of 12 would be reduced somewhat, probably to about 10 times earnings. Scott, on the other hand, expressed his belief that investors would not be averse to Crimmins Equipment's use of more debt, with the result that the current price-earnings ratio would not be changed.[3]

To aid him in making the final decision, Crimmins asked Fitzgibbons to prepare a set of tables for presentation at the next directors' meeting. Fitzgibbons proceeded along the following lines.

---

[2] The industry-average debt ratio is 50 percent and the average times interest earned is 7 times.

[3] The price/earnings ratio is the market price per share divided by earnings per share. It represents the amount of money an investor is willing to pay for $1 of current earnings. The higher the riskiness of a stock, the lower its P/E ratio, other things remaining constant.

Questions

1. Calculate earnings per share on the assumption that total sales are zero, $500,000, $2 million, $4 million, $6 million, $8 million, and $10 million. For purposes of making this calculation, Fitzgibbons assumed that fixed costs, not including interest, were $400,000 and that variable costs were 80 percent of sales.
2. Determine the breakeven sales level for earnings per share.
3. Determine market price per share at each level of sales if (a) debt or (b) equity financing is used, and the breakeven sales level for market price.
4. Graph the earnings and price figures to facilitate presentation to the board.
5. The probability distribution for various sales levels has been estimated by the marketing department as follows:

Sales Level:	$. 0	$2 million	$4 million	$6 million	$8 million	$10 million
Probability:	.01	.14	.35	.35	.14	.01

What is the expected EPS under each financing method?

6. The standard deviation of expected earnings under bond financing is $1.92, and under equity financing $1.27. How might Fitzgibbons evaluate the two alternatives using this information?
7. Fitzgibbons calculated the firm's expected combined leverage factor (from last year's approximate sales level of $4 million), assuming bond financing, to be 5.0, and he claimed that if sales could be increased from last year's $4 million level to $10 million next year, this 150 percent increase would lead to a 750 percent (5.0×150) increase in earnings. If last year's total asset turnover is a good indicator of the firm's production ability at full capacity, and if this ratio is not expected to increase next year, is Fitzgibbons' claim valid?
8. Prepare a verbal statement of the good and bad aspects of the two financing proposals and make a recommendation as to which one should be accepted.

Table 11.1

CRIMMINS EQUIPMENT COMPANY
INCOME STATEMENT FOR YEAR ENDED DECEMBER 31
(in thousands)

	1972	1971
Sales	$4,200	$3,900
Total costs (excluding interest)	3,560	3,410
Net income before taxes	$ 640	$ 490
Debt interest (6%)	90	90
Income before taxes	$ 550	$ 400
Taxes	275	200
Net income	$ 275	$ 200

Table 11.2

CRIMMINS EQUIPMENT COMPANY
BALANCE SHEET, DECEMBER 31
(in thousands)

	1972	1971
ASSETS		
Current assets	$1,400	$1,200
Net fixed assets	1,920	1,820
Other assets	430	400
Total	$3,750	$3,420
LIABILITIES		
Current liabilities	$ 450	$ 310
Long-term debt (6%)	1,500	1,500
Common stock, $5 par	500	500
Earned surplus	1,300	1,110
Total	$3,750	$3,420

Westgate Hardware Company

(Valuation)

Martin Turner, 47 years of age, has just retired after 30 years in the U.S. Navy. He enjoyed the service, but his wife and two teenage daughters disliked the periodic moves Navy men must make.

Turner's last 20 years have been spent operating ships' stores and post exchanges on Navy bases. During this time he gained considerable experience in operating and managing general merchandise and small appliance departments, and he has accumulated a net worth of approximately $110,000, of which $10,000 is on deposit in a savings and loan association and $100,000 is invested in a portfolio of high-quality common stocks. In addition, Turner's pension provides him with payments of approximately $400 per month. Enjoying good health, he has no intention of "being put out to pasture." Rather, Turner is interested in purchasing and operating the Westgate Hardware Company, a medium-sized hardware store in a Los Angeles suburban shopping center.

Westgate Hardware was established in 1952 by Lionel James and was operated by him until his death in 1967. James' widow has run the store from 1968 to the present time, 1972, but the profits of the business have been much lower under her management than they were under her husband's. Her principal problems have been (1) a tendency to stock higher-quality and more expensive items than should be carried, given the income characteristics of the shopping center's patrons, and (2) a tendency to be too lenient in granting credit and too lax in collecting past-due accounts. As a result, the investment in inventories and accounts receivable has been excessive, and losses on accounts receivable have further reduced the store's profitability. Mrs. James is reluctant to give up the store, but her own health is failing and she feels that if she receives a good offer, she should sell out.

Soon after he learned about the possibility of buying Westgate Hardware through a wholesale appliance salesman, one of his suppliers when he was running the small appliance department at the San Diego Naval Base Exchange, Turner met Mrs. James and made a careful investigation of the situation. From his discussion with Mrs. James' banker, several wholesale hardware salesmen, and proprietors of other stores in the shopping center, Turner concluded that the Westgate Store held a great deal of promise, but that Mrs. James was simply not running it properly. With his experience, Turner felt that he would be able to do considerably better.

Table 12.1 shows the balance sheet for Westgate Hardware as of December 31, 1972. Table 12.2 shows the sales and profits before taxes for the 11-year period 1962 through 1972. Turner concluded, on the basis of a physical examination, that both the fixed assets and the inventories shown on the balance sheet were fairly valued. He was somewhat more skeptical about the accounts receivable; Mrs. James has been allowing extended terms for the purchase of more expensive appliances, and a number of the accounts appear to be past due.

In his investigation, Turner learned that the neighborhood around the shopping center had been built up by the end of the 1950s; therefore, the shopping center could not expect to attract additional patrons, and any growth in sales would be because of rising personal incomes or, possibly, because patrons of the shopping center could be induced to buy more of their hardware locally rather than through downtown stores. Although growth potential was limited, Turner also learned that no new hardware

Table   12.1

WESTGATE HARDWARE COMPANY
DECEMBER 31, 1972

Cash	$10,800	Accounts payable	$5,400
Accounts receivable	18,000	Other current liability	900
Inventories	43,200		
Furniture, fixtures, and equipment, less reserve for depreciation	18,000	Common stock plus earned surplus	83,700
Total assets	$90,000	Total liabilities and net worth	$90,000

Table   12.2

WESTGATE HARDWARE COMPANY
SALES AND PROFITS BEFORE TAXES, 1962–1972

Year	Sales	Profit before Taxes[a]
1962	$71,100	$7,110
1963	74,700	7,560
1964	77,400	7,560
1965	81,000	7,920
1966	83,700	8,190
1967	82,800	7,740
1968	78,300	3,060
1969	74,700	3,420
1970	81,900	3,690
1971	84,600	3,240
1972	80,100	3,330

[a] Mrs. James' tax rate is about 15 percent.

stores could open in the shopping center and that, because of limited facilities, it was highly unlikely that any new hardware stores could open close enough to compete with Westgate Hardware within the local area.

When they discussed a possible sales price, Mrs. James indicated that she was willing to sell the store for $90,000, but that she would withdraw the $10,800 now held in cash before turning over the store to Turner.

Questions

1. If Turner purchases the Westgate Hardware Company, what will his total investment be? Be sure to include any additional investment outlays that will be required over and above the purchase price. For purposes of the question, assume the purchase price will be $90,000. (See Table 12.3.)

2. If Turner asked you to make "high," "low," and "most likely" estimates of annual profits after he takes over the store, what estimates would you reach? Assume (1) that Turner will set up the store as a corporation, but (2) that he will elect to be taxed as a proprietorship, (3) that the tax rate on the store's income will be 25 percent, and (4) that he will withdraw all profits for personal expenditures without paying additional taxes.

3. Using the after-tax profit estimates you obtained in (2), calculate

Table 12.3

STANDARD STATISTICS
ON MEDIUM-SIZED HARDWARE STORES, 1972
(percentages)

Cash	8.0	Accounts payable	12.0
Accounts receivable	16.0	Bank loans	25.0
Inventories	54.0	Total current liabilities	37.0
Total current assets	78.0	Long-term debt	15.0
Fixed assets[a]	22.0	Common stock plus surplus	48.0
Total assets	100.0	Total liabilities and net worth	100.0

[a] Assumes building rented, not owned.

maximum, minimum, and "most reasonable" prices that Turner might pay for the store.

4. What is the minimum price that Mrs. James should accept for the store?
5. If Mrs. James holds out for $90,000, should Turner purchase the store?

Brower Lumber Company

(Valuation)

The Brower Lumber Company was organized in 1920 by Daniel Brower to exploit the growing demand for California redwood lumber products. The company was profitable and grew steadily during the 1920s, but it had a difficult time surviving during the depression years of the 1930s. However, since 1938 Brower Lumber Company has shown a profit in every year.

Until his retirement in 1961 at the age of 70, Daniel Brower, the founder, owned 100 percent of the company's common stock. He then sold 15 percent of the shares to Ellis Porter, his assistant, who took over active management of the firm. Brower retained the remaining 85 percent of the stock. In the 10 years since Porter began to run the company, Brower Lumber has experienced the fastest rate of growth and most profitable operations in its 50-year history.

When Daniel Brower died in March 1972, he left a sizable estate, but he also left a difficult problem: determining the exact value of the estate for use in establishing the estate tax. Avery Adams, the federal estate tax appraiser assigned to the case, reported a tentative value of $3,825,000 for the common stock in Brower Lumber Company owned by Brower at the time of his death. In his report, this figure was calculated by multiplying 85 percent of the $300,000 earnings available to common stock of the company (Table 13.1) by a price-earnings factor of 15.0.[1] Ernest Wayburn, the attorney representing Mrs. Brower and the estate, took exception to Adams' figure, stating that Brower's interest in the estate should be based on book value. On this basis, the estate had a value of $2,330,000, figured as 85 percent of the net worth of Brower Lumber Company (Table 13.2).

Thus, the difference between the two estimates of the value of the

Table 13.1

BROWER LUMBER COMPANY
YEAR ENDED DECEMBER 31, 1971

Sales	$2,300,000
Cost of goods sold	1,386,000
General and administrative expenses	170,000
Interest: Notes $ 4,000	
Bonds 80,000	84,000
Profit before taxes	$ 660,000
State and federal income taxes	330,000
Profit after taxes	$ 330,000
Preferred dividends	30,000
Net income for common stock	$ 300,000
Dividends	150,000
Addition to retained earnings	$ 150,000

Table 13.2

BROWER LUMBER COMPANY
DECEMBER 31, 1971

Cash and marketable securities	$ 139,000	Accounts payable	$ 71,000
Accounts receivable	417,000	Notes payable (9%)	53,000
Inventories	824,000	Other current liabilities	34,000
Total current assets	$1,380,000	Total current liabilities	$ 158,000
Plant and equipment (net)	$1,420,000	Long-term debt (4%)	$2,000,000
		Preferred stock (6%)	500,000
		Common stock ($1 par)	100,000
Timber reserves (cost)	$2,600,000	Retained Earnings	2,642,000
	$5,400,000		$5,400,000

---

[1] The price-earnings ratio simply indicates how much investors are willing to pay for $1 of earnings.

estate is $1,495,000. In view of the fact that the marginal estate tax rate for estates of the approximate size of Brower's, whatever it turns out to be, is about 50 percent, the estate tax payable under Adams' valuation is approximately $747,000 greater than it is under Wayburn's valuation. Because of the magnitude of the sums involved, Mrs. Brower has authorized Wayburn not only to argue with the tax people, but also to take the case to court if a satisfactory compromise cannot be reached.

In an effort to strengthen his case, Wayburn retained Dr. Barry Phillips, Professor of Finance at the University of Northern California, as an independent outside expert on corporate valuation. Phillips has been given a briefing on the problem and has been asked to determine a fair value for the company. Wayburn supplied Phillips with the income statement in Table 13.1 and the balance sheet in Table 13.2. Phillips also examined older balance sheets and income statements, but he determined that the 1971 statements are typical of statements for the last 10 years with regard to the key ratios and the like. Phillips did, however, develop the statistics shown in Table 13.3 in order to gain some idea of the firm's rate of growth over the past decade.

Wayburn asked Phillips to develop his best estimate of the true value of the company, as well as high and low ranges. He requested, "Give me your best judgment as to the true and proper value of the firm. Also, I would like a high estimate—the maximum figure that we should consider as being at all acceptable—and the lowest valuation figure that the tax people are likely to accept. I will, naturally, try to reach a compromise with them as close as possible to the low figure, but I am equally sure that they will be going for the high one. At any rate, I need some reference points when I bargain with the tax boys."

Wayburn also asked Phillips if the book value he used as an estimate

Table   13.3

BROWER LUMBER COMPANY
SALES, EARNINGS PER SHARE, AND DIVIDENDS,
1961–1971

Year	Sales	Earnings per Share	Dividends per Share
1971	$2,300,000	$3.00	$1.50
1970	2,165,000	2.71	1.50
1969	1,942,000	2.56	1.75
1968	1,257,000	1.38	1.50
1967	1,900,000	2.48	1.25
1966	1,567,000	2.04	1.00
1965	1,400,000	1.76	.85
1964	1,160,000	1.50	.70
1963	1,400,000	1.67	.70
1962	1,020,000	1.23	.70
1961	1,065,000	1.39	.70

of the true value of the firm might not be overstating the value of the estate. Wayburn reasoned that the book value of the company's common stock is, if anything, overstated relative to market value because interest rates at the present time are very much higher than they were when the long-term debt and the preferred stock were sold to an insurance company. Wayburn pointed out that the presently outstanding long-term debt, which will not mature for another 30 years, carries a 4 percent interest rate, whereas new debt, if it were sold in today's market, would carry an 8½ percent interest rate. Similarly, the preferred stock, which has no maturity date, would have a 9 percent yield if it were sold today. These changed interest rate conditions, according to Wayburn, should cause the book value of the common stock to be higher than its "true" value.

Finally, Wayburn sent Phillips the statistics on Arcadia and Sierra lumber companies given in Table 13.4. These two companies are more similar to Brower Lumber Company than any other companies whose stocks are traded in the public market. However, they are both considerably larger than Brower Lumber Company, Sierra being about 5 times and Arcadia about 20 times the size of Brower (size is measured by assets). Wayburn guessed that Avery Adams probably had found his price-earnings ratio of 15 from one or the other of these two companies, but he argued that because of the size differentials between these companies and Brower Lumber Company, such comparisons were inappropriate.

Questions

1. If you were in Phillips' position, what would be your estimates of the high, low, and "best" valuation for Brower Lumber Company? Justify your figures as fully as possible.
2. Do you agree with Wayburn's point about the effect of changing interest rates on the value of the common equity?
3. Can you see why the estate tax is frequently given as one of the dominant reasons for privately held companies going public?

Table 13.4

ARCADIA AND SIERRA LUMBER COMPANIES

	Arcadia	Sierra
Earnings per share: 1971	$ 1.65	$ 2.45
Earnings per share: 1966	1.25	1.85
Dividends per share: 1971	1.20	1.98
Dividends per share: 1966	0.91	1.48
Book value per share: 1971	16.00	25.00
Market price per share: December 31, 1971	25.00	34.00

W. H. Girsch Company

(Cost of Capital)

The W. H. Girsch Company, which was founded in 1909, is a leading producer of such household hardware items as curtain and drapery rods, picture hangers, and the like. The company's home office and largest manufacturing facilities are located in the Cleveland area, and additional manufacturing facilities are located in Los Angeles, Houston, and Atlanta. The company has been prosperous throughout its 60-year history, but its most significant growth occurred during the 1950s and 1960s.

Girsch was operated as a closely held, family-owned corporation until 1962, when approximately 20 percent of the outstanding stock was sold to the general public by the descendants of W. H. Girsch. Since the original public offering, members of the family have disposed of an additional 50 percent of the stock. Therefore, in 1972, 30 percent of the shares are still held by the family and 70 percent are owned by outsiders.

The firm was controlled by members of the Girsch family until 1971, when W. H. Girsch, II retired from active participation in its affairs. Since no other member of the family was interested in or qualified to assume a dominant role in management, Rex Wiley, Vice President of McWilliams and Company, a national consulting firm, was brought in as president and chief executive officer. He did, however, bring Raleigh Todd, a 28-year-ple in production, marketing, personnel, and so on—to be excellent, so he did not institute any major personnel changes upon his takeover as chief executive officer. He did, however, bring Raleigh Todd, a 28-year-old M.B.A. who had been with McWilliams and Company for about five years, with him as assistant to the president. Todd's primary responsibility was to seek out weaknesses in Girsch's operating and administrative procedures and to devise methods for strengthening these weaknesses.

One of the first things Todd noticed was the rather haphazard manner in which capital investment decisions were reached. For the most part, capital budgeting decisions seemed to be made by Charles Cromwell, Financial Vice President, without any systematic analysis. Apparently, Cromwell simply approved all requests for capital expenditures as they were made by the different departments. However, Cromwell did periodically review the rate of return on investment in the different departments, and if the rate of return for a given department was seriously below that of the firm as a whole, the department head was notified that his results were below average.

As a result of this procedure, heads of departments with below-standard returns tended not to make substantial requests for expansion funds until their departments' returns were brought up to the average of the firm.

It was apparent to Todd that this informal procedure tended to cause available funds to be allocated to departments with the highest return on investment. Todd also noted that during years when expansion had been more rapid than normal, such as in 1966 and 1969, Cromwell had requested information on the payback period for the larger capital expenditure proposals, rejecting several proposals on the grounds that (1) the firm was short of funds for additional capital expenditures and (2) the payback on the rejected projects was relatively low compared to that on certain other available projects.

In early 1973 Todd wrote a memorandum to Wiley, with copies sent to the other major executives of the firm (the executive committee), suggesting that the capital budgeting process be formalized. Specifically, Todd recommended that the firm adopt the net present value approach, whereby projects are first ranked in accordance with their net present values and then all projects with positive net present values are accepted.

The proposal was enthusiastically endorsed by Wiley, but Todd detected a certain amount of skepticism about the proposal on the part of the other senior officers, especially Cromwell. Although Cromwell seemed to endorse the principle of using a present value approach to the capital budgeting decision, he was skeptical about the ability of the firm to find an appropriate discount rate, or cost of capital, to use in the capital budgeting process.

Todd was directed by the executive committee to develop a cost of capital for the firm to use in evaluating 1973 capital investment decisions. As a first step in this task, he obtained the most recent balance sheet (Table

14.1), as well as information on sales and earnings for the past 11 years (Table 14.2). In addition, Todd had discussions with several investment bankers and security analysts for major brokerage firms to learn something about investor expectations for the company and about the costs that would be incurred by the firm if it attempted to obtain additional outside

Table   14.1

W. H. GIRSCH COMPANY
December 31, 1972 (thousands)

Cash and marketable securities	$ 2,500	Accounts payable[a]	$ 200
Accounts receivable	18,600	Bank notes payable (8%)	7,000
Inventories	21,200	Other current liabilities	500
Total current assets	$42,300	Total current liabilities	$ 7,700
Net fixed assets	27,700	Long-term debt (5%)	8,000
		Preferred stock (6%)	3,500
		Common stock[b]	50,800
	$70,000		$70,000

[a] Accounts payable are exceptionally low because the firm follows the practice of paying cash on delivery in exchange for substantial purchase discounts.
[b] There are 1,000,000 shares outstanding.

Table   14.2

W. H. GIRSCH COMPANY
Sales and Earnings, 1962–1972

Year	Sales	Earnings after Taxes Available to Common Stock[a]
	(millions)	
1972	$105.2	$5,312,000
1971	103.1	5,064,000
1970	91.8	4,713,000
1969	78.2	4,391,000
1968	69.9	3,982,000
1967	56.5	3,517,000
1966	54.2	3,166,000
1965	51.3	2,623,000
1964	38.1	2,210,000
1963	33.7	1,963,000
1962	31.9	1,708,000

[a] The firm's marginal tax rate is 50 percent.

capital. From the security analysts Todd received the impression that investors do not expect W. H. Girsch Company to continue to enjoy the same rate of growth it has enjoyed over the past 10 years. In fact, most of the analysts seemed to be estimating its future growth to be about half the rate experienced during the last decade. The analysts, however, do expect the firm to continue paying out about half its earnings available to common in the form of cash dividends. In the last annual meeting, Wiley, indeed, announced that the policy of paying out at least 50 percent of those earnings would be maintained. Wiley also stated that if expansion needs did not require the 50 percent retention rate, the payout ratio would be increased.

Todd learned that the company could obtain additional long-term debt from life insurance companies at an interest rate of approximately 8 percent. Also, additional short-term debt funds could be obtained from commercial banks at this same rate. Both of these rates assume that Girsch's financial position as measured by its debt ratio would not decline.

The company's preferred stock, which has no maturity since it is a perpetual issue, pays a $6 annual dividend on its $100 par value and is currently selling for $70 a share. The investment bankers informed Todd that additional preferred stock could be sold to provide investors with the same yield as is available on the current preferred stock, but they added that flotation costs would amount to $2 a share. In other words, if the company were to sell a preferred stock issue paying a $6 annual dividend, investors would pay $70 a share, the flotation cost would be $2 a share, so the company would net $68 a share.

The company's common stock is currently selling for $60 a share. The investment bankers informed Todd that additional shares could be sold at 5 percent discount from the current price, or at about $57 a share. In other words, the investment bankers feel that they can sell additional shares to the public at $60, and they will keep $3 a share for their efforts, thus netting Girsch $57 a share.

Todd anticipates some sharp questioning when he presents his estimate of the firm's cost of capital. Accordingly, he is resolved to make as complete and careful a study of the subject as possible. From his preliminary discussions with Wiley, Todd concludes that he should discuss the questions that follow in his report.

Questions

1. Todd estimates that 1973 earnings available to common will be $5,500,000. With the continuation of the current dividend policy (a payout of at least 50 percent), this indicates that the 1973 dividend will be $2.75. Given the existing capital structure, what is the marginal cost of capital if net assets grow at each of the follow-

ing rates during the coming year: (a) 2 percent, (b) 5 percent, (c) 10 percent, (d) 20 percent? (Use short-term debt but disregard accounts payable or other current liabilities in computing the capital structure. Also, for purposes of answering this question, assume that investors' long-run expectations about growth in earnings and dividends would not be affected by one-year changes in the rate of growth in assets, that is, k is independent of the 1973 asset growth rate.)

2. If interest rates on long-term debt declined from the current 8 percent level to 5 percent, how would this affect (a) the marginal and average cost of debt capital, (b) the marginal and average cost of equity capital, and (c) the overall marginal and average cost of capital? Do you think this change would affect the optimal capital structure? (No calculations required.)

3. Suppose the company uses additional capital for investments in projects with a higher degree of risk than is inherent in the existing assets. What effect would this have on the firm's cost of capital?

4. What effect would changing the capital structure to include more debt have on (a) the cost of debt, (b) the cost of equity, and (c) the overall cost of capital?

5. Suppose Todd learns from the investment bankers that if Girsch sells more than $2 million of new debt during 1973, its interest cost on this new debt will rise from 8 percent to 12 percent, and any debt above $4 million will cost 15 percent, assuming the present capital structure is maintained. In addition, assume that the firm has four major investment opportunities available to it in the near future:

Project	Cost	Project's IRR
A	$6 million	10.00 percent
B	$4 million	9.10 percent
C	$8 million	10.25 percent
D	$4 million	9.25 percent
E	Purchase Marketable Securities	9.00 percent

a. Graph the firm's marginal cost of capital (MMC) and marginal rate of return (IRR) curves.

b. Which projects should Todd recommend?

c. Discuss the breaking points on the MCC curve. What factors would, in reality, tend to smooth out the curve?

6. Todd is considering recommending a change in the firm's capital structure to include more debt. Although the situation cannot be quantified precisely, Todd believes that the return demanded by

stockholders, k, is a function of (1) the after-tax riskless interest rate, i, currently about 4 percent, (2) a premium demanded of the firm as a result of its particular business activity, γ, currently about 8 percent for W. H. Girsch Company, and (3) a premium demanded as a result of the firm's financial leverage, β. Todd believes that this last figure can be approximated by taking the firm's debt ratio (Debt/Assets), squaring it, and multiplying by .10 to give the additional percentage points of premium required by the market $(\beta = (D/A)^2 \, (.10))$. Todd feels that the firm's cost of debt is also a function of the debt ratio, and that this function is approximately equal to the following schedule:

Ratio Debt/Assets	After-tax Cost of Debt
0%	.04
10.0%	.04
20.0%	.04
30.0%	.05
40.0%	.06
50.0%	.08
60.0%	.10
70.0%	.13

Assuming that the firm has only debt and common stock in its capital structure, what is the approximate optimal debt ratio? (HINT: Solve graphically.)

Wisconsin Electric Power Company

(Cost of Capital)

BACKGROUND ON UTILITY REGULATION

A large segment of the U.S. economy, including electric and gas distribution companies and telephone and other communications firms, as well as railroads, airlines, and bus companies, is regulated to some extent. Economies of scale in these industries require that only one or a relatively few large firms serve each market if production costs are to be minimized. Utility companies are, therefore, given franchises to operate in specified areas.

Regulatory bodies generally set the prices charged by public utilities. Since utilities are granted franchises to provide essential services, competition among firms is limited in comparison with other industries. Further, because the service is essential, demand is relatively inelastic. With inelastic demand and limited competition, the firms would be in an ideal position to exploit their markets were it not for price regulations. For this reason, most utilities are regulated, with the prescribed rates being just sufficient to provide companies a "fair" return on investment.

In theory, the regulatory procedure calls for estimating the demand and cost schedules under normal conditions and then using these two schedules to produce estimates of profits at various prices. These relationships are illustrated in Figure 15.1. At a price P^*, Q^* units are demanded.

The cost per unit at Q^* units of output is C^*. The profit per unit is equal to $P^* - C^*$, and this unit profit, multiplied by Q^* units, gives total profits. Under normal conditions, a higher price results in greater profits due to the price inelasticity of demand.

Profit plus interest payments plus preferred dividends is the total return investors receive on their investment. If this total return is divided by total investment—the commitment of investors—we obtain the rate of return on investors' capital. The rate of return on total capital should be equal to the weighted average cost of capital. Preferred dividends and interest payments are fixed, as is total capital (or the rate base). There-fore, the profits available to common stock is the decision variable, and given the desired rate of return on investment, the utility commission knows approximately how large profit should be. Further, given cost and demand schedules, the commission can set the particular price that pro-duces the desired level of profits. For example, if investment (the rate base) is $100 million, preferred dividends and interest charges are each

Figure   15.1

HYPOTHETICAL DEMAND-COST RELATIONSHIPS
FOR A UTILITY COMPANY

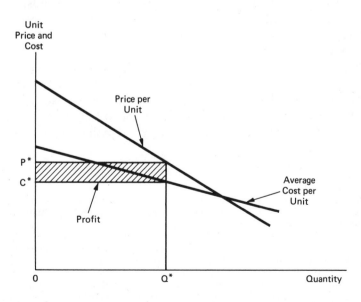

$1 million, and the allowed rate of return is 6.5 percent, the profits should total $4.5 million.[1]

Actually, utility regulation is not nearly so rigid as this simplified discussion suggests. For one thing, most regulators recognize that such rigidity, even if it were possible, would leave little or no room for managerial incentive—the profit motive would be totally removed if the companies were simply guaranteed a specified profit. As a result, rates are set sufficiently low so that companies must strive to keep costs down and demand up in order to attain the profit goal. Further, rates are changed with a lag. If a particular company is especially efficient and thus able to keep its cost lower than those used when the rate schedule was set, then it will be able to earn a higher than prescribed rate of return—at least until the regulatory agency orders a rate reduction. Conversely, if costs rise and profits fall, there will be a lag before a rate increase can be obtained. This lag also provides a powerful stimulus to efficiency.

Thus, the regulatory process for utilities calls for (1) determining the rate base or the invested capital upon which the rate of return is earned and (2) determining a fair rate of return, defined by the Supreme Court in the Hope Natural Gas Company case as a rate of return high enough to permit the company to raise the funds it needs for expansion while, at the same time, maintaining the financial integrity of the enterprise. It was stated in the Hope case that these conditions would be met if companies earned rates of return commensurate with the returns enjoyed by other companies having corresponding risks. In other words, if XYZ Electric Company has a degree of risk σ, and if other companies with this same degree of riskiness earn 10 percent on their assets, XYZ should also be allowed to earn 10 percent.

The problem, thus, is to determine the utility's *average* cost of capital and to set prices such that the company earns this rate of return on its entire investment.[2] The general procedure is to find the average cost of debt and preferred stock, as well as the current cost of equity capital, and then to find a weighted cost of capital, using the capital structure weighted

---

[1] This example is grossly simplified in order to indicate the concepts involved without getting lost in details. In the first place, the cost and demand schedules are impossible to determine exactly. Further, the actual size of the rate base is subject to dispute. Finally, utilities serve several classes of customers; this means that a number of different demand schedules with varying price elasticities are involved, and therefore, any number of different rate schedules could be used to produce the desired level of profits.

[2] Note that it is the average, not the marginal, cost of capital that is critical in utility cases because the return allowed is on the entire plant, not just new additions. Therefore, if a company obtained long-term debt or preferred stock at a time when interest rates were low, this lowers the average cost of capital. New, higher interest rates (marginal cost of debt) affect only the average cost of debt over time as expensive debt replaces cheap debt.

by book values of each capital component.[3] The cost of debt and preferred stock is seldom a controversial issue, but the cost of equity is always troublesome. In general, the utility companies prefer to determine equity capital costs by analyzing the rate of return on book value of equity (earnings/book value of common equity), while regulatory agencies are beginning to adopt the Gordon approach of measuring the cost of equity as the dividend yield plus an expected growth rate.[4] Predictably, returns on book value generally exceed the cost of capital as determined by the Gordon approach.

WISCONSIN ELECTRIC POWER

On July 12, 1968, the Wisconsin Electric Power Company filed an application to increase rates for electric service with the Public Service Commission of Wisconsin. The application stated that the company was seeking reasonable and just rates which would produce sufficient revenues to meet its operating expenses, yield a fair return on capital, and insure Wisconsin Power's ability to attract the capital necessary to finance power plants and facilities under construction.

Wisconsin Electric Power Company serves the general area of southeastern Wisconsin, including Milwaukee and the surrounding suburbs. To meet anticipated future power requirements, Wisconsin Power and its wholly owned subsidiary, Wisconsin Michigan Power Company, are constructing a nuclear power plant. Because of this and other projects, the company plans a construction program involving expenditures of approximately $232 million in the four-year period 1970–1973. To finance this program, Wisconsin Power will need substantial amounts of both new equity and debt capital.

Hearings were held on January 12, 1969, and testimony with respect to the rate of return Wisconsin Power should receive was presented on behalf of the company by A. Gruhl, Chairman of the Board, and by J. Kingsland, Vice President of White, Weld and Company (an investment

---

[3] Note that the cost of debt is the return investors receive. Therefore, no tax adjustment is needed for the cost of debt for utilities as is the case for unregulated firms.

[4] Myron Gordon was consultant to the Federal Communications Commission during 1966–1967 in connection with a major study of American Telephone & Telegraph's price structure. Gordon applied his basic model to AT & T in an effort to determine the cost of equity capital to AT & T. Subsequently, other regulatory agencies picked up this same line of thought. It should also be noted that while AT & T's capital structure consisted of 33 percent debt and 67 percent equity, Gordon argued that an optimal capital structure for the company should have about 50 percent debt. He further argued that the FCC should, in effect, force AT & T to use more debt by using a 50 percent debt ratio in calculating the cost of capital. This calculation, as presented by Gordon, would have resulted in a lower cost of capital than if the more conservative debt position were to be maintained. AT & T actually did agree to use more debt in the future, indicating that academic research has had at least some impact on corporate practices!

banking firm), and on behalf of the Public Service Commission by C. F. Huebner, Director, Utility Accounts and Finance Division. It was generally agreed among the three men that the firm's two issues of preferred stock (5 percent of total capital) had an annual cost of 3.95 percent and that the 12 outstanding issues of first mortgage bonds or debentures (56 percent of total capital) had an annual cost of 4.94 percent. However, varying views were expressed with respect to the cost of common stock equity, which comprised approximately 39 percent of Wisconsin Power's total capital as of December 31, 1968.

Gruhl concluded that a 12 percent return should be allowed on common stock equity. His conclusion was based on an analysis of the latest available earnings of the middle third of a group of 60 other utility companies operating in the United States. The average rate of return on book value of equity of this middle third was 12 percent, and Gruhl felt that his firm was comparable in risk with these 20 companies. Kingsland's testimony, in which he concluded that a return of not less than 12 percent on common stock was required, was based primarily on his computation that the company should have earnings sufficient to cover interest charges by at least 2.8 times—a generally accepted minimum coverage used by long-term lenders. Any return on equity less than 12 percent would cause the interest coverage figure to fall below 2.8 times.

The staff witness employed several approaches to determine a cost of equity capital to Wisconsin Power. First, Huebner noted that since 1949 the company has marketed nine separate issues of common stock sold at an average cost of 8.8 percent, where cost is measured by the ratio of the earnings per share at the time of issue to the net proceeds per share (earnings per share divided by stock price less flotation costs). Second, Huebner conducted a test aimed at giving some indication of the market expectations of the company's stockholders based on average dividend yields and growth in book value per share.[5] This analysis indicated a cost of common stock for recent periods of approximately 9.75 percent. Finally, Huebner showed that Wisconsin Power's 10-year average of earnings as a percent of common stock book value was 10.3 percent. The same figure for 18 large manufacturing firms located in Wisconsin was 9.28 percent. Huebner concluded that the appropriate cost of equity is 9.75 percent, a figure that represents a compromise between his high and low estimates.

Table 15.1 shows the estimated operating income (earnings after taxes but before interest, or earnings available to common and preferred stock plus interest), for 1969 as computed by the company assuming the present rate, or price, structure. Table 15.2 shows the company's average rate base.

---

[5] This test employed the so-called Colbert formula, a model similar in nature to the Gordon model, that is frequently used in public utility cases.

Table 15.1

ESTIMATED INCOME STATEMENT, WISCONSIN ELECTRIC
12 Months Ending June 30, 1969

Operating revenue	$173,000,000
Operating expenses	
Operation and maintenance	$ 80,420,000
Depreciation expense	17,150,000
Taxes other than income tax	17,213,000
Federal income taxes	19,195,000
State income taxes	2,545,000
Total	$136,523,000
Operating income	$ 36,477,000[a]

[a] Operating income divided by rate base equals rate of return.

Table 15.2

AVERAGE NET INVESTMENT RATE BASE,
WISCONSIN ELECTRIC
12 Months Ending June 30, 1969

Utility plant in service	$693,190,000
Deduct: Reserve for depreciation	187,270,000
Retirement work in progress	(300,000)
Contributions in aid of construction	1,450,000
Total	$188,420,000
Net utility plant in service	$504,770,000
Add: Materials and supplies	20,840,000
Prepayments	450,000
Cash working capital requirement	5,900,000
Construction work in progress	49,660,000
Net investment rate base	$581,620,000

Questions

1. What figures should the Public Service Commission use for cost of (a) equity capital, (b) debt, and (c) preferred stock? (NOTE: *Do not* use an after-tax cost of debt. The figure given has already been adjusted for taxes.)
2. Using (a) 11 percent and (b) 9.75 percent as the cost of equity, calculate the weighted average cost of capital for Wisconsin Electric Power Company. What is the dollar difference in operating revenues under each of these assumptions? If no rate increase is

granted, what will Wisconsin Electric Power Company's estimated rate of return be?

3. If the Public Service Commission wère to order the company to increase its debt to 75 percent, and to lower common equity to 20 percent, what effect would this have on the weighted average cost of capital?

4. Suppose that over a number of years interest rates rose dramatically on long-term debt—say from 5 percent on new debt to 8½ percent on new debt (because of increase in the demand for debt funds relative to the supply of such funds, *not* because of increased riskiness of debt). What effect would this have on the firm's (a) cost of debt as used in rate cases, (b) cost of equity (HINT: think of the "riskless rate + risk premium concept"), and (c) average cost of capital?

5. Is the projected rate of growth in assets a significant factor in the cost of capital determination for Wisconsin Power Company? That is, would the average cost of capital be significantly different if the growth in assets was (a) zero or (b) 50 percent per year?

6. What are the major differences in the cost of capital for utilities versus industrial companies with regard to (a) the calculation of the cost of capital and (b) the use of the cost of capital figure developed?

7. Can you think of any uses of the public utility concepts of the cost of capital by major aerospace firms engaged in defense work such as General Dynamics and North American-Rockwell?

Questions to be assigned at the option of the instructor:

8. Interpret your answer to question 3 in terms of the theoretical proposition of Modigliani-Miller.

9. Given that the cost of equity is a function of the riskless interest rate plus premiums for the firm's business and financial risk:

$$k = i + (\beta + \gamma) = i + P$$

a. How would cost of equity be affected by the determination that Wisconsin Electric Power Company's earnings had a regression coefficient ("beta") with the market's earnings of $b = -1.0$? of $b = 0$? of $b = +1.0$? of $b = +2.0$? of $b = 0.7$?

b. Which situation would generally be most likely for a public utility company?

c. Should the rate regulation hearings have attempted to determine and evaluate information of this sort before making its decision?

Renk Petroleum Company

(Dividend Policy)

The Renk Petroleum Company was established in 1933 by Jonathan Renk, an independent oil producer who acquired the assets of a number of bankrupt oil companies during the early years of the depression. Renk recognized the growing demand for petroleum products and, under his direction, the company aggressively sought new oil reserves both by acquisitions and through its own explorations. The company made two major strikes, one off the Louisiana coastline in 1953 and another in Indonesia in 1966. While Renk Petroleum is not one of the giants of the industry, it is extremely well endowed with oil reserves relative to its own refining and marketing capacity. This excellent reserve position has put the company in a favorable position to expand its refinery facilities and retail outlets during the 1970s.

Jonathan Renk has always operated the firm in an aggressive manner. His policies have paid off in rapid growth in sales and assets, but this rapid growth, in turn, has produced some acute financial problems. The extent of these problems is revealed by an examination of Table 16.1, which shows condensed balance sheets for 1950, 1960, and 1970. It can be seen from Table 16.1 that the debt ratio rose from 30 to 50 percent over the 20-year period; the current ratio declined from 5 to 1 to only 1.6 to 1; and the cash to current liabilities ratio declined from 1.5 to 1 in 1950 to only 0.14 to 1 on December 31, 1970.

Table   16.1

RENK PETROLEUM COMPANY
YEAR ENDED DECEMBER 31
(in millions)

	1950	1960	1970
Cash and marketable securities	$ 18.3	$ 31.7	$ 17.5
Accounts receivable	25.8	51.8	126.3
Inventories	17.1	26.5	54.6
Total current assets	$ 61.2	$110.0	$198.4
Fixed assets (net)	54.6	193.5	589.6
Total assets	$115.8	$303.5	$788.0
Current liabilities	$ 12.3	$ 31.4	$124.0
Long-term debt	22.5	90.0	270.0
Common equity	81.0	182.1	394.0
Total liabilities and net worth	$115.8	$303.5	$788.0
Current ratio (2.7 to 1)[a]	5 to 1	3.5 to 1	1.6 to 1
Cash to current liabilities (1.0 to 1)[a]	1.5 to 1	1.0 to 1	0.14 to 1
Debt ratio (28%)[a]	30%	40%	50%

[a] The numbers in parentheses represent industry averages, which were stable over the period covered.

Jonathan Renk and members of his immediate family owned 75 percent of Renk Petroleum's stock in 1950. By 1970, because of the issuance of shares to acquire new companies, the need to sell common stock to raise funds for expansion, and his gifts to charitable foundations, Renk's ownership position had declined to only 35 percent of the outstanding stock.

The company has never paid a cash dividend, nor has it ever declared a stock dividend or had a stock split. Jonathan Renk has always taken the position that the firm needs to retain all of its earnings to help finance its expansion program and, on that basis, he has followed a policy of paying no cash dividends. It is his opinion that both stock dividends and stock splits are pointless—in his words, "They merely divide the pie into smaller slices." Renk also thinks that stock dividends or stock splits would increase the costs to the company of processing the additional pieces of paper. And finally, since the stock is listed on the New York Stock Exchange and since the commission, as a percentage of the transaction, is higher on large purchases of lower-priced stocks than on higher-priced ones, a stock split or dividend would increase stockholders' transfer costs.

At the annual stockholders' meeting in April 1971, a number of very vocal stockholders expressed disapproval of the firm's past dividend policy.

One stockholder made a passionate speech in which he pointed out that while earnings in 1970 amounted to $130 a share, while the book value of equity per share—most of which was represented by retained earnings—was over $1,800, and while the president of the company's salary and other benefits for 1970 amounted to over $200,000, the stockholders received a zero dividend for the 37th consecutive year. When other stockholders joined in the chorus, Jonathan Renk, Chairman of the Board, and Timothy Cramden, President, recognized that they had the makings of a stockholder revolt on their hands. Since rumors were currently circulating around Wall Street that two large conglomerates were considering making tender offers for Renk Petroleum stock, management was anxious to keep stockholders as happy as possible. Accordingly, Renk announced to the group that not only would he call a special meeting of the board of directors within the next month to consider the dividend policy but also that he would announce the results of the meeting to stockholders in the next quarterly newsletter.

In the special directors' meeting, it was immediately apparent that the directors were divided into four groups. The first group, headed by Renk, felt that while a cash dividend would appease certain stockholders, such a dividend was out of the question. Renk pointed to the balance sheet as dramatic proof of this position.

Charles Wilson, an investment banker whose firm represented many small stockholders, expressed his view that a cash dividend was definitely indicated and also that a sizable stock split was in order. Several other directors agreed with Wilson that a cash dividend was necessary, but they preferred a stock dividend as opposed to a stock split.

The fourth group of directors agreed that cash dividends should be paid as soon as possible—even if it meant a cutback in the company's expansion plans—and contended also that a sizable stock split or stock dividend should be declared at once. This group went even further, however, and recommended that the company should announce a large stock split immediately and that thereafter the company should follow a practice of declaring quarterly stock dividends with a value approximately equal to earnings retained during the quarter. In other words, if the firm earned $2 a share during a given quarter and paid a cash dividend of $1, then this group would have the company declare a stock dividend of a percentage equal to $1 divided by the market price of the stock. For example, if the stock was selling for $50 a share at the time the $1 stock dividend was declared, then a 2 percent stock dividend would be distributed.

Since there was a prevailing belief among many of the stockholders that Renk's position was a result of his desire to avoid paying income taxes on cash dividends, this fourth group made the additional proposal that, as an alternative to cash dividends, the firm might consider a share repurchase plan, under which the distribution would take the form of a capital gain which could be realized or not realized at the discretion of the shareholder.

After an extended discussion, it became apparent that the directors were too widely split to reach a decision at that time; therefore, another meeting was called for the following week. Warren Heeman, Financial Vice President, was directed to evaluate the four positions expressed at the meeting and to recommend a dividend policy to the board the following week.

Just as he was beginning to map out his research strategy for the hurried report, Heeman received a memorandum from Patrick Benish, Sales Manager and a member of the board. Benish supplied Heeman with the figures shown in Table 16.2, and added a short note asking Heeman to consider whether or not the firm's dividend policy and position on stock splits might have had an effect on the price of the company's stock relative to the prices of other stocks.

Questions

1. What is the significance, if any, of the data presented in Table 16.2?

Table   16.2

RENK PETROLEUM COMPANY

Year	Earnings per Share	Book Value per Share	Average Market Price per Share	Price-Earnings Ratios, Industry Average	Market Value-Book Value Ratio, Industry Average
1970	$130	$1,818	$1,566	16 times	2.5 times
1965	98	1,543	1,278	19 times	2.9 times
1960	94	1,215	1,110	18 times	2.6 times
1955	85	1,035	1,010	17 times	2.5 times
1950	58	810	580	10 times	1.2 times

Period	Growth in Earnings, Industry Average
1965–1970	8%
1960–1965	7%
1955–1960	6%
1950–1955	7%

2. Evaluate each of the four positions taken by the different groups of directors.

3. Make a recommendation and be prepared to defend it against alternative proposals as to a desirable cash dividend and stock dividend and/or stock split policy for Renk Petroleum. Be sure to specify how large the stock split should be, if a stock split is employed, or how large the stock dividend should be if this procedure is followed.

Eastern Industries, Inc.

(Dividend Policy)

The management of Eastern Mills, Inc., a textile milling concern, made a decision in 1955 to diversify into areas with greater growth potential than textiles. While growth possibilities were distinctly limited in the textile field, Eastern Mills was generating substantial cash flows from profits and depreciation every year. Under the diversification plan, these cash surpluses would be used to buy firms in high-technology growth industries. In addition, since in 1955 Eastern Mills had a relatively small amount of debt outstanding, it planned to use debt financing in its acquisition program. When the plan was put into operation, some of the acquisitions were made with cash generated from internal operations, some with cash obtained through the sale of stock or bonds by Eastern, and some by Eastern's exchanging its own securities—generally either common stock, convertible bonds, or convertible preferred stock—for the stock of the acquired company.

At the beginning of 1956, all of the assets of the company were invested in textile operations. By the end of 1971, however, textiles amounted to only 50 percent of assets, sales, and income, with the other 50 percent coming from new divisions in such fields as the manufacture of computer peripheral equipment, electronic components, and similar growth-oriented products. To reflect the diversified nature of its business, in 1960 the name of the company was changed from Eastern Mills to Eastern Industries.

The company has followed a practice of paying out two-thirds of earnings as cash dividends for the past 40 years. Accordingly, dividends have fluctuated with earnings from year to year. In each annual report, the policy of paying out two-thirds of earnings has been restated, and this policy of a generous dividend is one of the hallmarks of Eastern Industries. Because of the firm's generous dividend policy, Eastern Industries stock is owned by retired individuals, college endowment funds, income-oriented mutual funds, and other investors seeking a stable source of income. Surveys taken by the company clearly indicate that its present stockholder list is dominated by income-seeking investors. Further, it is significant to note that not one single growth-oriented mutual fund owns Eastern Industries stock.

Until the January 1972 directors' meeting, at which directors traditionally have considered plans for the coming year, dividend policy was never discussed; it was simply assumed that the policy of a payout of two-thirds would be maintained. At the January 15, 1972, meeting, however, Robert Rhet, Vice President of the Space Systems Division and a man brought into the company when the firm he had founded merged with Eastern Industries, stated that the dividend policy should be examined. Rhet reasoned that while a high dividend payout might have been a desirable policy for the company when it had poor internal growth potentials, it is totally inappropriate for a firm with growth opportunities as good as those now available to Eastern Industries. Rhet pointed out that capital limitations had recently forced the firm to turn down some capital investment opportunities that promised relatively high rates of return. He also indicated that he and several other directors who had large holdings of the firm's stock were paying approximately 75 percent of all dividends received to state and federal governments in the form of income taxes. If the company retained most of its earnings, this would be reflected in the price of the stock, and should he or other large stockholders desire to obtain cash, they could sell some of their shares and be taxed at a capital gains tax rate of 25 percent rather than at the 75 percent tax rate on dividends.

Ellis Porter, Treasurer of Eastern Industries, strongly supported Rhet's suggestion that dividends be reduced. Porter declared that the firm's current ratio had deteriorated from a level of about 5 in 1956 to only 1.6 in 1971 and that the debt ratio had risen from only 16 percent in 1956 to almost 58 percent in 1971. Responsible for dealing with banks, insurance companies, and other lenders, he reported a reluctance on the part of these credit sources to continue making funds available to Eastern Industries if the debt and liquidity ratios continued to deteriorate. Porter offered the figures shown in Table 17.1 to illustrate his position.

Table   17.1

EASTERN INDUSTRIES, INC.
YEAR ENDED DECEMBER 31
(in millions)

	1956	1971
Current assets	$18.0	$242.4
Fixed assets	29.2	278.2
	$47.2	$520.6
Accounts payable	$ 0.8	$ 65.3
Notes payable	1.6	71.0
Other current liabilities	1.2	15.2
Total current liabilities	$ 3.6	$151.5
Long-term debt: Nonconvertible	4.0	75.0
Long-term debt: Convertible	—	75.0
Common equity: Common stock ($1 par)	5.6	19.9
Surplus (capital and earned)	34.0	199.2
Total liabilities and net worth	$47.2	$520.6
Current ratio	5 to 1	1.6 to 1
Debt ratio	16%	57.9%

Phillip Morgan, trustee of the endowment trust of a major university and a long-term member of the Eastern Industries board, took exception to the positions of Rhet and Porter. Morgan contended that the firm had followed a consistent dividend policy for many years and that present stockholders had made their purchases of the stock on the assumption that this policy would be continued. Also, he reported that the results of a questionnaire sent out with the last dividend check revealed that stockholders show an overwhelming preference for a policy of high dividends as opposed to a policy of low dividends. Morgan stated that because of its acute need for current income, his university's trust fund would be forced to sell its Eastern Industries stock if the dividend was cut significantly. Morgan was sure that a number of other institutional holders would react similarly and, from answers to the questionnaires sent to individual stockholders, he believed many of them would also sell their stock in the event of a sizable dividend cut. According to Morgan, these liquidations of Eastern Industries stock from so many portfolios would have a disastrous effect on its price.

At this point, Porter, Secretary as well as Treasurer, stated that he had to agree with Morgan's arguments. As Secretary, Porter handled correspondence with stockholders. In this capacity, he had gained a very distinct impression that the majority of stockholders did indeed want dividends and would, in fact, sell their holdings if dividends were eliminated or reduced materially.

Avery Cohen, Manager of the Data Systems Division and, like Rhet, brought into Eastern Industries when his own firm was acquired, joined the discussion in favor of the payout reduction. Cohen argued that the company's dividend policy was responsible for the type of stockholders the firm has. He suggested that had the firm retained all of its earnings rather than paying two-thirds of them out in dividends, acquisitions could have been made for cash rather than by issuing new stock. With fewer shares of stock outstanding, earnings per share would be higher today and would have shown a higher growth rate over the past decade. This higher growth rate, according to Cohen, would have induced growth-oriented institutional and individual investors to purchase Eastern Industries stock. Cohen concluded by saying that he believed the high dividend policy in past years was a mistake, but a mistake that could be rectified by changing the policy at the present time. He discounted the argument that the price of the stock would be depressed if the dividend was cut. Rather, Cohen argued that aggressive investors would more than take up the slack caused by possible liquidations of income-seeking investors, with the result that the price of the stock would increase, not decrease, if dividends were cut.

The discussion continued for almost an hour past the scheduled adjournment time and terminated only because Morgan had to catch a plane. Before adjourning, however, the board directed Jarvis Stearns, Vice-President, Finance, to study the whole question of dividend policy and to make a report at the next directors' meeting, scheduled to be held in one month. Stearns was given explicit directions to study the following alternative policies:

1. A continuation of the present policy.
2. A policy of lowering the present payout to some percentage below 67 percent (for example, 20, 30, or 40 percent) and then maintaining the payout ratio relatively constant at this new figure.
3. Establishing a dollar amount of dividends, say $1 a year, and maintaining the dividend at this rate. As earnings fluctuate, the dividend payout ratio would fluctuate. Eventually, the dollar dividend would be increased, assuming earnings continue to rise. If this policy is adopted, the question of the initial dividend, in relation to current earnings (the payout ratio), must also be settled.
4. Setting a relatively low dividend payout, say 50 cents a share, then supplementing this regular dividend with an extra dividend that would depend on the availability of funds and the need for capital. Again, the matter of total payout would arise.

The directors also requested Stearns to consider the question of whether or not the dividend policy, whatever was decided upon, should be announced. Rhet and Cohen both expressed the opinion that dividend policy should not be announced, citing the company's present position as an example of how an announced policy can cause the firm to feel "locked in" and force it to take actions that otherwise would be undesirable.

As Stearns was leaving the meeting, Cohen also asked him to include in his report an analysis of the firm's past growth rates in sales, total earnings, and earnings per share and some statement of how the earnings per share figures might have differed had the firm followed a different payout policy. (See Table 17.2)

Table   17.2

EASTERN INDUSTRIES, INC.

Year	Sales (millions)	Earnings after Taxes (millions)	Earnings per Share	Dividends per Share	Average Stock Price during Year
1971	$782.3	$43.8	$2.20	$1.47	$33.00
1966	438.6	25.6	1.80	1.20	30.50
1961	226.1	12.9	1.41	.94	28.25
1956	70.8	2.8	0.50	.33	6.25

Cohen promised to send Stearns some figures on payout ratios and price-earnings ratios which he had seen in a brokerage house report a few days before. These figures are given in Table 17.3.

Table   17.3

	Payout Ratio	Price-Earnings Ratio
Carter Electronics	0%	83 times
Data Systems	0%	63 times
Xerox	18%	47 times
IBM	20%	38 times
U.S. Tobacco	90%	9 times
Collins Coal	70%	14 times
AT & T	60%	13 times
Midwest Electric	80%	12 times

Questions

1. Evaluate the advantages and disadvantages of each of the four dividend policies mentioned above. Consider the policies as they apply to the case of Eastern Industries. Use a hypothetical graph showing internal rate of return schedules and a cost of capital schedule to illustrate your analysis.
2. Evaluate the advantages and disadvantages of having an announced dividend policy.
3. What effect does the payout policy have on the growth rate of earnings per share?
4. Could the figures shown in Table 17.3 be considered proof that firms with low payout ratios have high price-earnings ratios? Justify your answer.
5. How does the firm's debt position affect the dividend decision?
6. Evaluate Cohen's argument that a reduction in the dividend payout rate would increase the price of the stock versus Morgan's opinion that such a reduction would drastically reduce the price of the stock.
7. Might stock dividends be of use here?
8. What specific dividend policy should Stearns recommend to the board at its next meeting?

Part IV

Long-term External Financing

Seavers Components Corporation

(Investment Banking)

In March 1970, three executives of the Hughes Aircraft Company, one of the largest privately owned corporations in the world, decided to break away from Hughes and to set up a company of their own. The principal reason for this decision was capital gains; Hughes Aircraft stock is all privately owned, and the corporate structure makes it impossible for executives to be granted stock purchase options. Hughes' executives receive substantial salaries and bonuses, but this income is all taxable at normal tax rates, and no capital gains opportunities are available.

The three men, Tom Mathis, Rex Chalk, and Sid Ashley, have located a medium-sized electronics manufacturing company available for purchase. The stock of this firm, Seavers Components Corporation, is all owned by the founder, Bernard Seavers. Although the company is in excellent shape, Seavers wants to sell it because of his failing health. A price of $4,800,000, based on a price-earnings ratio of 12 and annual earnings of $400,000, has been established. Seavers has given the three prospective purchasers an option to purchase the company for the agreed price, the option to run for six months, during which time the three men are to arrange financing with which to buy the firm.

Mathis has contacted John McCall, a partner in the New York investment banking firm of Barnes, Stern and Company and an acquaintance of some years' standing, to seek his aid in obtaining the funds necessary to complete the purchase. Mathis, Chalk, and Ashley each have some money available to put into the new enterprise, but they need a substantial amount of outside capital. There is some possibility of borrowing part of the money, but McCall has discouraged this idea. His reasoning is, first, that Seavers Components is already highly leveraged, and if the purchasers were to borrow additional funds, there would be a very severe risk that they would be unable to service this debt in the event of a recession in the electronics industry. Although the firm is currently earning $400,000 a year, this figure could quickly turn into a loss in the event of a few canceled defense contracts or cost miscalculations.

McCall's second reason for discouraging a loan is that Mathis, Chalk, and Ashley plan not only to operate Seavers Components and seek internal growth but also to use the corporation as a vehicle for making further acquisitions of electronics companies. This being the case, McCall believes that it would be wise for the company to keep any borrowing potential in reserve for use in later acquisitions.

McCall proposes that the three partners obtain funds to purchase Seavers Components in accordance with the figures shown in Table 18.1.

Seavers Components would be reorganized with an authorized five million shares, with one million to be issued at the time the transfer takes

Table 18.1

SEAVERS COMPONENTS CORPORATION

Price paid to Seavers		$4,800,000
(12 × $400,000 earnings)		
Authorized shares	5,000,000	
Initially issued shares	1,000,000	
Initial distribution of shares:		
Mathis	80,000 shares at $1.00	$ 80,000
Chalk	80,000 shares at $1.00	80,000
Ashley	80,000 shares at $1.00	80,000
Barnes, Stern and Co.	100,000 shares at $6.50	650,000
Public stockholders	660,000 shares at $6.50	4,290,000
	1,000,000	$5,180,000
Underwriting costs: 5% of $4,290,000	$214,500	
Legal fees, and so on, associated with issue	35,500	$ 250,000
		$4,930,000
Payment to Seavers		4,800,000
Net funds to Seavers Components		$ 130,000

place and the other four million to be held in reserve for possible issuance in connection with acquisitions. Mathis, Chalk, and Ashley would each purchase 80,000 shares at a price of $1 a share, the par value. Barnes, Stern and Company would purchase 100,000 shares at a price of $6.50. The remaining 660,000 shares would be sold to the public at a price of $6.50 a share.

Barnes, Stern and Company's underwriting fee would be 5 percent of the shares sold to the public, or $214,500. Legal fees, accounting fees, and other charges associated with the issue would amount to $35,500, for a total underwriting cost of $250,000. After deducting the underwriting charges and the payment to Seavers from the gross proceeds of the stock sale, the reorganized Seavers Components Corporation would receive funds in the amount of $130,000, which would be used for internal expansion purposes.

As a part of the initial agreement, Mathis, Chalk, and Ashley each would be given options to purchase an additional 80,000 shares at a price of $6.50 a share. Barnes, Stern and Company would be given an option to purchase an additional 100,000 shares at $6.50 a share.

Questions

1. What is the total underwriting charge, expressed as a percentage of the funds raised by the underwriter? Does this charge seem reasonable in the light of published statistics on the cost of floating new issues of common stock?

2. Suppose that the three men estimate the following probabilities for the firm's stock price one year from now:

Price	Probability
$ 0	.05
4	.10
8	.35
12	.35
16	.10
20	.05

Assuming Barnes, Stern and Company exercises its options, calculate the following ratio (ignore time-discount effects):

$$\frac{\text{Total return to Barnes, Stern and Company}}{\text{Funds raised by Underwriter}}$$

Disregard Barnes, Stern & Company's profit on the 100,000 shares it bought outright at the initial offering. Comment on the ratio.

3.   Are Mathis, Chalk, and Ashley purchasing their stock at a "fair" price? Should the prospectus disclose the fact that they would buy their stock at $1 a share, whereas public stockholders would buy their stock at $6.50 a share?

4.   Would it be reasonable for Barnes, Stern and Company to purchase its initial 100,000 shares at a price of $1?

5.   Do you forsee any problems of control for Mathis, Chalk, and Ashley?

6.   Would the expectation of an exceptionally large need for investment funds next year be a relevant consideration when deciding upon the amount of funds to be raised now?

Fidelity Savings and Loan

(Decision To Go Public)

Fidelity Savings and Loan Association was organized in 1953 in Bellwood, California, a suburb of Los Angeles. The area has grown rapidly, its population increasing from 23,000 in 1953 to 178,000 in 1971. Per capita incomes in Bellwood are substantially above the average for California, and savings per capita is likewise well above the state average. The combination of an increasing population, high savings per capita, and a huge demand for funds to finance new home construction has made Fidelity Savings and Loan the most rapidly growing association in the state, in terms of both assets and earnings.

Fidelity's rapid expansion has put the company under a severe financial strain. Even though it is very profitable and earnings have been increasing at a rapid pace—and all earnings have been retained—the net worth to assets ratio has been declining substantially until, by 1971, it is just above the minimum required by the California Savings and Loan Commissioner. (See Table 19.1)

Fidelity Savings and Loan now has the opportunity of opening a branch office in a new shopping center. If the office is opened, it will bring in profitable new loans and deposits, further increasing the association's growth. However, an inflow of deposits at the present time would cause the net worth to assets ratio to fall below the minimum requirement. Accordingly, Fidelity must raise additional equity funds if it

Table   19.1

FIDELITY SAVINGS AND LOAN
December 31, 1971[a]

Assets	
Cash and marketable securities	$ 24,186,000
Mortgage loans	236,300,000
Fixed assets	17,514,000
Total assets	$278,000,000

Liabilities	
Savings accounts	$236,856,000
Other liabilities	24,186,000
Capital stock ($100 par)	300,000
Earned surplus	16,658,000
	$278,000,000

[a] Figures and account titles modified.

NOTE: State law requires the ratio of capital plus surplus to assets to be at least 6 percent.

is to open the new branch.

Although Fidelity has a ten-man board of directors, the company is completely dominated by the three founders and major stockholders—Howard Edmonton, Chairman of the Board and owner of 35 percent of the stock; Mark Tamper, President and owner of 35 percent of the stock; and Harold Arnoldson, a builder serving as a director of the company, who owns 20 percent of the stock. The remaining 10 percent of the stock is owned by the other seven directors. Arnoldson and Edmonton both have substantial outside financial interests; the majority of Tamper's net worth is represented by his stock in Fidelity Savings and Loan.

Edmonton, Tamper, and Arnoldson agree that Fidelity should obtain the additional equity funds to make possible the branch expansion. However, they are not in complete agreement as to how the additional funds should be procured. They could raise the additional capital—the required amount is approximately $1 million—by having Fidelity Savings and Loan sell newly issued shares to a few of their friends and associates. The other alternative is to sell shares to the general public. The three men cannot, themselves, put additional funds into the company at the present time.

Edmonton favors the private sale. He points out that he, Tamper, and Arnoldson have all been receiving substantial amounts of ancillary, or indirect, income from the savings and loan operation. The three men jointly own a holding company which operates an insurance agency that writes insurance on many of the homes financed by Fidelity Savings and Loan; a title insurance company that deals with the association; and a construction company that obtains loans from the association. In addition, Arnoldson's construction company occasionally borrows substantial amounts from Fidelity. Edmonton maintains that these arrangements could be continued without serious problems if the new capital were raised by selling shares to a few individuals, but conflict of interest problems might arise if stock were sold to the general public. He is also opposed to the public offering on the grounds that the flotation cost would be high for a public sale, but would be virtually zero if the new stock were sold to a few individual investors.

Tamper disagrees with Edmonton; he feels that it would be preferable to sell the stock to the general public rather than to a limited number of investors. Acknowledging that flotation costs on the public offering are a consideration and that conflict of interest problems may occur if shares of the company are sold to the general public, he argues that several advantages would accrue if the stock is publicly traded: (1) The existence of a market-determined price would make it simpler for the present stockholders to borrow money, using their shares in Fidelity Savings and Loan as collateral for loans. (2) The existence of a public market would make it possible for current shareholders to sell some of their shares on the market if they needed cash for any reason. (3) Having the stock publicly traded would make executive stock option plans more attractive to key employees of the company. (4) Establishing a market price for the shares would simplify problems of estate tax evaluation in the event of the death of one of the present stockholders. (5) Selling stock at the present time would facilitate additional stock sales in the future if growth required the procurement of additional equity capital.

Arnoldson, whose 20 percent ownership of the company gives him the power to cast the deciding vote, is unsure whether he should back the public sale or the private offering. He thinks that additional information is needed to help clarify the issues.

Questions

1. Table 19.1 presents Fidelity Savings and Loan's balance sheet at the end of 1971. Using information contained in the balance sheet, calculate the number of shares of stock outstanding and the book value per share of common stock.
2. Since Fidelity's assets and liabilities are fixed-value financial items, book values for companies in this industry are more meaningful than book values of many industrial firms. Accordingly, book values are given substantial weight when determining market prices of savings and loan association stocks. During 1971, the stock of rapidly growing savings and loan associations generally sold in the vicinity of twice the book value. Assuming the two

times book value multiple is applicable for Fidelity, what would the market value per share of the company be?

3. Investment bankers generally like to offer the stock of companies that are going public for the first time at a price ranging from $10 to $30 a share. If Fidelity stock were to be offered to the public at a price of $15 a share, how large a stock split would be required prior to the sale?

4. Assume Fidelity chooses to raise $1 million through the sale of stock to the public at $15 per share. (a) Approximately how large would the percentage flotation cost be for such an issue? Base your answer on available published statistics. (b) How many shares of stock would have to be sold in order for Fidelity to pay the flotation cost and receive $1 million net proceeds from the offering?

5. Assume that each of the three major stockholders decided to sell half of his stock. (a) How many shares of stock and what total amount of money (assuming the stock split occurs and these shares will be sold at a price of $15 per share) would be involved in this secondary offering? (A secondary offering is defined as the sale of stock that is already issued and outstanding. The proceeds of such offerings accrue to the individual owners of the stock that is sold in the secondary offering, not to the company.) (b) Approximately what percentage flotation cost would be involved if the investment bankers were to combine the major stockholders' secondary offering with the sale by the company of sufficient stock to provide it with $1 million?

6. Assume that the major stockholders decide that Fidelity should go public. Outline in detail the sequence of events—from the first negotiations with an investment banker to the receipt of the proceeds of the offering by Fidelity Savings and Loan.

7. Can you see why Edmonton and Tamper might have personal differences on the question of public ownership?

8. All things considered, do you feel that Fidelity Savings and Loan should go public? Justify your conclusion.

USM Corporation and McWilliams Oil

(Pre-emptive Right, Cumulative Voting)

Large, publicly owned corporations are required to solicit proxies prior to their annual meetings. Listed on the notice of meeting are the names of the candidates management proposes for election as directors of the corporation. In addition, the notice summarizes the major issues scheduled for discussion at the meeting, such as proposals to merge with other companies, proposals to issue new common stock, stock option plans for corporate executives, and so on. Stockholders are notified of the time and place of the annual meeting and are informed that they may attend the meeting and vote their shares in person.

The notice of the annual meeting and statement of proposed actions are accompanied by a proxy, or ballot, in the form of an IBM card. On the card are the major proposals, with boxes for checking a "for" or "against" vote. The most important item on the proxy statement is the request that stockholders give their rights to vote at the annual meeting to one or more individuals designated on the proxy statement. If a stockholder checks the appropriate slot, signs the statement, and returns it to the company, then he has given his proxy to a management delegate. If the stockholder changes his mind at any time prior to the meeting, he may sign a new proxy statement or appear at the meeting, void his old proxy statement, and vote in person as he sees fit on the various issues.

Normally, stockholders give their proxies to management and vote on different issues in accordance with management recommendations. Occasionally, however, disagreements occur, and what is known as a proxy fight breaks out. A proxy fight can develop over any type of issue, but the most common causes are proposals for mergers with other firms and proposals by dissident stockholders to institute changes in the management of a company on the grounds that the present management is not doing as good a job as could be done by some other group.

In addition to these major proxy battles, there are occasionally some minor squabbles. Frequently these relatively minor arguments are brought on by what might be called professional stockholders. These are a small number of relatively wealthy individuals who buy a few shares in each of a large number of major corporations. They then use the proxy mechanism to attempt to institute certain reforms—or changes which they consider to be reforms—in major publicly owned corporations. The professional stockholders are, in a sense, crusaders for the rights of the small stockholders. There is, however, some difference of opinion as to the merits of the professional stockholders' positions.

The two points over which management and the professional stockholders most frequently disagree are (1) the existence of the pre-emptive right and (2) cumulative voting. The first topic is discussed in the USM case, the second in the McWilliams Oil case.

USM CORPORATION

The following is an excerpt from the *USM Corporation Notice of Stockholder Meeting* for 1969:

IV. STOCKHOLDER'S PROPOSAL ON
PRE-EMPTIVE RIGHTS
Mrs. Margaret R. Gilbert, 1165 Park Avenue, New York, New York, who states that she is the owner of 40 shares, and represents an additional family interest of 200 shares, of Common Stock of the Corporation, has notified the Corporation that she will introduce from the floor at the annual meeting the following resolution:

RESOLVED: That the stockholders of USM Corporation, assembled in annual meeting in person and by proxy, hereby request that the Board of Directors take the steps necessary to restore limited pre-emptive rights to the shareholders.

Mrs. Gilbert has submitted the following statement in support of her proposal:

Last year management requested the elimination of pre-emptive rights. When new stock issues are floated by a corporation the dollar of the continuing owner is worth just as much as the dollar of the newcomer and a minimum underwriting fee arrangement can net more to the corporation.

Companies recently taking this step include: Xerox, General Motors, Philip Morris, U. S. Steel and Chesebrough Ponds.

If you agree, please mark your proxy FOR this resolution; otherwise it is automatically cast against it.

The Board of Directors and the management recommend that the stockholders vote AGAINST this proposal, for the following reasons:

At the 1968 Annual Meeting, the Corporation's stockholders approved an amendment of the Corporation's Certificate of Incorporation which, among other things, eliminated pre-emptive rights with respect to Common Stock. (Holders of the Corporation's Preferred and Preference Stock have never had pre-emptive rights.) Of the total votes cast by stockholders, approximately 97% of the shares voted by holders of Common Stock and 96% of the shares voted by holders of 6% Preferred Stock were voted for this amendment.

As stated in the Proxy Statement for last year's Annual Meeting, the Board of Directors believes that the absence of pre-emptive rights of holders of the Common Stock will be helpful in financing expansion of the Corporation's business and will eliminate delay, expense and uncertainty which would exist if every issuance of stock which might be deemed to be for cash had to be first offered to the holders of Common Stock of the Corporation. The Board of Directors believes that limited pre-emptive rights do not benefit the stockholders as a whole and that they do not necessarily provide the least expensive means by which an individual stockholder can preserve his equity position.

The board also considers that pre-emptive rights have less significance today in the case of a corporation whose shares are publicly held, actively traded and listed on a national stock exchange than was the case in the past when shares of many corporations were closely held. Stockholders interested in continuing their proportionate holdings in a publicly held corporation normally can do so by purchases on the open market.

The Corporation is organized under the laws of the State of New Jersey. Effective January 1, 1969, the New Jersey Business Corporation Act completely revised, simplified, clarified and modernized the New Jersey law governing corporations. The diminution in importance of pre-emptive rights is reflected in this Act. In the case of corporations newly organized under this statute, as well as under the Delaware General Corporation Law adopted in 1967, pre-emptive rights exist only if they are specifically conferred by the corporation's certificate of incorporation. Under the prior laws, pre-emptive rights existed unless they were expressly denied, limited or waived by the stockholders.

Questions

On the USM proxy card the above quotation is summarized and spaces are provided for stockholders to vote either for Mrs. Gilbert's proposal or against it. If you were a stockholder, how would you vote?

McWILLIAMS OIL COMPANY

The following is an excerpt from the McWilliams Oil Company *Notice of Stockholder Meeting* for 1969.

V. STOCKHOLDER'S PROPOSAL
ON CUMULATIVE VOTING

Mr. Edward Phillips, 227 Fox Bluff Road, Scarsdale, New York, who states that he is the owner of 50 shares of the Corporation's Common Stock, has notified the Corporation that he will introduce from the floor at the annual meeting the following resolution:

RESOLVED: That the stockholders of McWilliams Oil Corporation, assembled in annual meeting in person and by proxy, hereby request that the Board of Directors take the steps necessary to provide that the Corporation's Directors be elected on the basis of cumulative voting.

Mr. Phillips submitted the following statement to management in support of his proposal:

Cumulative voting for Directors is required in 22 of the 50 states including California, Illinois, Pennsylvania, Ohio, and Michigan. In our state of incorporation, Delaware, cumulative voting is not required, but many major Delaware corporations are providing for the election of Directors by the cumulative voting method.

The right of dissent is one of the cornerstones of our American heritage. If dissent is permitted, then all sides of an issue may be heard, and the rights of minority, as well as majority, interests may be voiced. It is just and equitable that minorities be given a voice in various matters affecting their well-being, and this right should extend to minority corporate stockholders.

The cumulative voting technique is designed to give representation to minority interests. In contrast, where cumulative voting is not used, only one group—management—is represented, and only one voice is heard.

The equitable, democratic way of electing Directors is by the cumulative voting method. If you agree, please mark your ballot FOR this resolution; otherwise your vote is automatically cast against the proposal.

The Board of Directors and the management recommend that the stockholders vote AGAINST this proposal, for the following reasons:

Your Corporation has, in the 53 years of its existence, grown to become one of the most profitable firms in the oil industry, indeed, in the nation. A recent survey of the 500 largest industrial firms rated your Corporation 23rd in growth of earnings per share over the past ten years and 14th in rate of return on invested capital. The price of your Company's stock reflects this outstanding performance.

We believe that management's performance record has been made possible by the *lack of dissent* among top management personnel. Since its foundation, your Corporation has believed in the principle of uniform goals and uniform policies at the top management level. We believe in discussing the pros and cons of a given issue and then reaching a conclusion on the issue. Once a conclusion has been reached, everyone in management—both those originally for the proposal and those against it —must assume that the decision is a good one and work to implement it.

It is your management's belief that cumulative voting will jeopardize the unity of purpose that has contributed so much to your Corporation's progress. Cumulative voting has, in other corporations, made it possible for minority interests to gain access to the Board of Directors and from this position to create dissent in an effort to change corporate policy. As a result, many formerly profitable and well-run corporations have suffered. We do not wish to see McWilliams Oil Corporation run the risk of experiencing a similar misfortune.

Accordingly, management requests that you vote *against* the proposal that the Corporation elect directors by the cumulative voting method.

Question

If you were a stockholder, would you vote for or against the proposal to elect directors by the cumulative voting method?

E. L. Edmonds Company

(Rights Offering)

E. L. Edmonds Company is the largest manufacturer of mobile homes in the nation. Organized in 1937, the company experienced a steady rate of growth in the post-World War II period. At first, its market consisted largely of vacationers and companies needing trailers for use at dam construction sites and in other areas where temporary housing was required. However, as the decade of the 1950s wore on, more and more mobile homes were produced for use as permanent residences, particularly for retired persons and young married couples. Sales of units for vacation homes were still strong during the fifties and sixties.

Recently, especially in 1969 and 1970, the demand for mobile homes has been increased by the effect of tight money on residential housing construction. The money drought and high interest rates that prevailed in 1969 and 1970 hit the housing industry harder than most other sectors of the economy, and, as a result, the construction of new housing units was curtailed during this period. The reduction in housing construction, combined with the new family formations caused by marriages among the members of the post-World War II "baby boom," has produced a serious housing shortage. In turn, this scarcity of conventional homes and apartments has stimulated the sale of mobile homes. They are much less expensive than the average house or apartment, and they can be financed through normal bank channels even when customary sources of mortgage funds have dried up.

To meet the increased demand, E. L. Edmonds is undertaking a major expansion program. A total of approximately $40 million in new capital over and above an expected $9 million of retained earnings is required for the years 1971 and 1972. Of this $40 million, $20 million has been borrowed from a group of five insurance companies on a long-term loan basis. The loan agreement, which has already been finalized, calls for E. L. Edmonds to raise an additional $20 million through the sale of common stock.

Edgar Edmonds, Chairman of the Board, Samuel Sherman, President, and Ronald Clarke, Vice President, Finance, are considering alternative ways of raising the $20 million of new equity funds. The firm's investment banker, Heard and Company, has informed Clarke that the following possibilities are available:

1. Edmonds could sell shares of stock directly to the public, not to stockholders, at a price of $96 a share. The company would net $91 a share, with $5 a share going to the investment banker as a commission. The current market price of the stock is $97, but the investment bankers anticipate that the price will decline temporarily to $96 as a result of the new shares coming on the market. The investment banker will, of course, promote the new issue in an effort to stimulate demand.

2. The company could sell shares to its stockholders at a price of $90 a share. Heard and Company would agree to guarantee the sale of the issue, and the commission would be $3 a share for every share subscribed to by stockholders and $7 a share for any shares left unsubscribed, which would be purchased by Heard and Company. In other words, if its stockholders subscribed to the full amount of the rights offering, Edmonds would receive $90 a share less a $3 commission, or a total of $87 a share. The proceeds of any unsubscribed shares would be $90 minus a $7 commission, or $83 a share.

3. Edmonds could sell stock through a rights offering at a price of $80 a share. Under this arrangement, the underwriting cost would be $1.50 for each share subscribed to and $7 for each unsubscribed share purchased by the investment banker.

4. Shares could be sold to current stockholders at a price of $50 a share. Under this arrangement, underwriting costs would be 50 cents a share for each share subscribed to by stockholders and $7 a share for each share taken by the investment banker.

5. Shares could be sold to current stockholders at $10 a share. Investment bankers would not be necessary under this proposal, as the

company could be quite sure that all shares offered would be taken.

Mr. Edmonds and Sherman have asked Clarke to prepare a report recommending which of the alternatives should be accepted or, if none of them is satisfactory, to suggest another alternative. In preparing his report, Clarke finds that the answers to the following questions are useful. (See also Tables 21.1 and 21.2.)

Questions

1. How many additional shares of stock would be sold under each of the proposals submitted by Heard and Company? (Assume all shares are subscribed.)
2. How many rights will be required to purchase one new share

Table   21.1
E. L. EDMONDS COMPANY
DECEMBER 31, 1970
(in millions)

Cash and marketable securities	$ 6.3
Accounts receivable	28.7
Inventories	32.8
Total current assets	$ 67.8
Fixed assets (net)	57.8
Total assets	$125.6
Accounts payable	$ 13.0
Bank loans (8%)	18.2
Total current liabilities	$ 31.2
Long-term debt (6%)	30.0
Capital stock (2 million shares outstanding)	15.0
Earned surplus	49.4
Total common equity	$ 64.4
Total liabilities and net worth	$125.6

Table   21.2

E. L. EDMONDS COMPANY

	1968	1969	1970
Total earnings after taxes (millions)	7.00	8.10	9.70
Total dividends paid (millions)	1.00	1.50	2.00
Market price per share (year-end)	75.50	85.25	97.00

under each of the proposals?

3. What is the market value of each right under each of the proposals? Do you think that the average stockholder would bother either to exercise his rights or to sell them at these prices? (Use the rights formula to answer this question.)

4. What will be the price per share immediately after issuance of the new shares under each of the four proposals? (Use the rights formula to answer this question.)

5. Selling stock through a rights offering with the subscription price set below the current market price has an effect that is similar to a stock split or stock dividend. What is the percentage of the stock dividend that would have to be declared to have the same effect—that is, produce the same final price per share—as each of the proposals for rights offerings?

6. Assume (a) that the company earns 9 percent after interest and taxes on total assets in 1971; (b) that the company obtains only $20 million of new equity financing during 1971, that is, the debt financing is deferred until 1972; (c) that new outside capital is fully employed during the entire year 1971; (d) that additions to retained earnings in 1971 are not employed until 1972; and (e) that current liabilities remain at their 1970 level. (Note that the company's stock issue was sold to the market for more than $20 million, but the investment bankers retained the difference to cover flotation charges; therefore, capital stock increases by exactly $20 million.) What will the rate of return on net worth, earnings per share, and the price of the stock (assuming a price-earnings ratio of 20) be in 1971 under each of the alternative financing methods? *Do not use the formula to answer this question.*

7. What are the maximum and minimum flotation costs under each of the proposals? Assume that the probability of the subscription percentage may be estimated by the following probabilities for maximum and minimum flotation costs:

Proposal	1	2	3	4	5
Probability maximum	—	.30	.20	.10	—
Probability minimum	—	.70	.80	.90	—

What are the expected flotation costs under each proposal?

8. What effects do you think a rights offering versus an offering to the general public would have on "stockholder loyalty" to the company?

9. Make a summary appraisal of each proposal and decide which method of financing Clarke should recommend to the board of directors.

Portland Electric Company

(Refunding a Bond Issue)

Darien Wycroft, Financial Vice President of Portland Electric Company, is reviewing the minutes of the last meeting of the firm's board of directors. The major topic discussed was whether or not Portland Electric should refund a $75 million issue of 26-year, 8 percent, first mortgage bonds issued 11 months previously. Three of the board members had taken markedly different positions on the question, and at the conclusion of the meeting William Pierpont, Chairman of the Board, requested Wycroft to prepare a report analyzing the alternative points of view.

The bonds in question had been issued the previous July, when interest rates were at their peak. Wycroft and the board of directors thought at the time that interest rates were at a high and were likely to decline in the future, but they had no idea that the slump would come so soon and be so sharp. Now, less than a year later, AAA utility bonds, such as those of Portland Electric, can be sold to yield only 6 percent.

Since Wycroft had anticipated a decline in interest rates when the $75 million issue was sold, he had insisted that the bonds be made immediately callable. The investment bankers handling the issue wanted Portland Electric to make the bonds noncallable for a five-year period, but Wycroft resisted this proposal. (If he had inserted the five-year call protection provision in the loan contract, the firm would have received an interest rate of approximately 7½ percent, one half of 1 percent less than the actual 8 percent.) The bankers, however, insisted on a call premium of 10 percent if any bonds were called during the first year, with the premium declining by ½ percent a year until the 20th year, after which the bonds could be called with no premium whatever.

Wycroft estimates that Portland Electric could sell a new issue of 25-year bonds at an interest rate of 6 percent. The call of old and sale of new bonds would take place in about five to seven weeks. The flotation cost on a refunding issue would be approximately ½ of 1 percent of the issue, and there would be a period of approximately two weeks during which both issues would be outstanding. He therefore proposed at the last directors' meeting that the company call the 8 percent bonds and refund them with a new 6 percent issue. Although the refunding cost would be substantial, he believes that the savings of 2 percent a year for 25 years on a $75 million issue would be well worth the refunding cost. Wycroft did not anticipate adverse reactions from the other board members, but three of them voiced strong opposition to the refunding proposal.

First, Warren Atwood, a long-term member of the board and Chairman of Atwood, Wilson & Company, an investment banking house catering mainly to institutional clients such as insurance companies, pension funds, and the like, argued that Portland Electric's calling the bonds for refunding would not be well received by the major financial institutions which hold the firm's outstanding bonds. Atwood pointed out that no utility, at least within his memory span, had called a bond issue in less than three years. According to Atwood, the institutional investors that hold the bonds had purchased them on the expectation of receiving the 8 percent interest rate for at least three years, and these investors would be very much disturbed by a call after only one year. Since most of the major lending institutions hold some of Portland Electric's bonds, and since the firm typically sells new bonds or common stocks to finance its growth every two or three years, it would be most unfortunate if institutional investors should develop a feeling of ill will toward the company.

Second, David Tucker, a relatively new member of the board and president of a local bank, also opposed the call, but for an entirely different reason. Tucker expressed the opinion that the decline in interest rates was not yet over. He stated that a survey by his bank suggested that the long-term interest rate might well fall as low as 5 percent within the next six months. Under questioning from other board members, however, Tucker admitted that the interest rate decline could in fact be over and that interest rates might, over the short term, move back up again.

Third, Charles Zwick, president of a management consulting firm specializing in utility operations, stated that while he was not opposed in principle to refunding operations, he questioned whether the proposed refunding would be profitable in view of (1) the very high call premium that would have to be incurred, (2) flotation costs on the refunding issue, and (3) the firm's 8 percent average cost of capital. Zwick suggested that a formal analysis using discounted cash flow techniques be employed to determine the feasibility of the refunding. As he thought over Zwick's proposal, Wycroft wondered whether, if the suggested procedure was followed, it might not be better to modify it by using Portland Electric's cost of debt rather than its average cost of capital. Further, if the cost of debt was used, he wondered if a before- or after-tax figure should be used.

Questions

1. Calculate the net present value of the savings assuming Portland Electric goes ahead with the refunding. Assume that the firm has a 50 percent marginal tax rate.
2. Give a critique of each of the positions expressed by various board members.
3. Should the refunding operation be undertaken at this time?

Potemkin Corporation

(Stocks versus Bonds)

The Potemkin Corporation is one of the largest manufacturers of plumbing supplies in the United States. The company was formed in 1927 as a consolidation of five smaller plumbing supply manufacturers, and, after experiencing severe difficulties during the 1930s, it grew steadily during the World War II era and throughout most of the post-war years. The company owes a large measure of its success to a patent on shower nozzles that was granted in 1939. Renewed in 1956, this patent is scheduled for final expiration in 1973.

During the years in which the shower nozzle patent has been in effect, Potemkin has enjoyed a virtual monopoly on shower and tub fixtures. The Justice Department instituted a suit against the company in 1947, charging that tie-in arrangements existed between it and large contractors and that Potemkin forced building contractors to take the firm's other products in order to obtain an uninterrupted supply of its shower nozzles. The charge was not substantiated, but the company certainly has received higher sales on other products than it would have had it not been for the shower nozzle.

When the shower nozzle patent expires in 1973, other plumbing manufacturers will be able to produce similar items and, accordingly, will subject Potemkin Corporation to intensified competitive pressures. Recognizing these impending developments, the firm has laid plans for a major modernization program to take place in 1972. The plan is designed to improve quality and to cut manufacturing costs and, thus, to enable the firm to meet the expected competition by offering better products at lower cost. If the modernization program is carried out, the Potemkin management team is confident that sales, profits, and the favorable trend in these two figures can be maintained at the same levels enjoyed during the decade of the 1960s.

In order to carry out the modernization program, Potemkin needs approximately $40 million of new external capital. The company has, ever since its founding, obtained all equity funds in the form of retained earnings. Short-term debt, in modest amounts, has been used on occasion, but no interest-bearing short-term debt is currently outstanding. The company borrowed $20 million at 4½ percent in 1960, but no additional long-term funds have been acquired since that date. (See Tables 23.1 and 23.2.)

Ralph Belcher, Vice President and Treasurer, must recommend a method of financing the required $40 million to the board of directors. In discussions with the firm's investment bankers, Belcher has learned that the funds may be obtained by three alternative methods:

1. The company could sell common stock to net $40 a share. Since the current price of the stock is $45 a share, a flotation cost of $5 a share is involved. The sale would be made through investment bankers to the general public; that is, the sale of common stocks would not be through a rights offering. The possibility of a rights offering was considered, but Belcher agreed with the investment bankers that the firm's currently outstanding common stock is not distributed sufficiently widely to insure the success of a rights

Table 23.1

POTEMKIN CORPORATION
DECEMBER 31, 1971
(in millions)

Current assets	$120
Fixed assets	190
Total	$310
Current liabilities (accruals and accounts payable)	$ 45
Long-term debt (4.5%)	20
Common stock ($1 par, 8 million shares outstanding)	8
Retained Earnings	237
Total liabilities and net worth	$310

Table 23.2

POTEMKIN CORPORATION
YEAR ENDED DECEMBER 31, 1971
(in millions)

Sales	$300.0
Cost of goods sold[a]	228.0
Gross profit	72.0
General and administrative expenses	7.0
Earnings before interest	65.0
Interest charges	.9
Earnings before taxes	64.1
Taxes (52% marginal rate)	33.3
Net income	30.8
Dividends	8.0
Addition to retained earnings	$ 22.8

[a] Includes depreciation charges of $15 million.

offering. The stock is traded over the counter, but at some future time the company will probably apply for listing on the New York Stock Exchange.

2. The company could sell privately 25-year, 8 percent bonds to a group of life insurance companies. The bonds would have a sinking fund calling for the retirement, by a lottery method, of 2 percent of the original amount of the bond issue each year. Covenants under the bond agreement would also require that dividends be paid only out of earnings subsequent to the bond issue; that is, the retained earnings of the company at present could not be used to pay dividends on the common stock. The bond agreement would also require that the current ratio be maintained at a level of at least 2 to 1, and the bonds would not be callable for a period of 10 years, after which the usual call premium would be invoked. No flotation costs would be incurred.

3. The third alternative available to the company is to sell 8 percent preferred stock. The issue would not be callable and would not have a sinking fund. The par value of the preferred stock would be $100 a share, the annual dividends would be $8 a share, and the stock would be sold to net the company $95 a share.

In preliminary discussions with Ezra Potemkin, Chairman of the Board, as well as its major stockholder, Belcher has learned that he favors the sale of bonds. Mr. Potemkin believes that inflation will continue for some years to come, so that the company will, by borrowing, be able to repay its loans with "cheap" dollars. In addition, the chairman notes that the firm's price-earnings ratio at present is relatively low, making the sale of common stock at this time unappealing. Finally, he notes that while his personal holdings are not sufficient to give him absolute control of the company, his shares, together with those of other members of his family and the other members of the board of directors, give management control of just over 50 percent of the outstanding stock. If additional shares are sold, management's absolute control will be endangered and the company will be subjected to the possibilities of a takeover by one of the major conglomerate companies. Finally, Potemkin notes that the after-tax cost of the bonds is relatively low and that the covenants should not prove onerous to the company.

Belcher has also discussed the financing alternatives with Bernard Swink, a long-term director and chairman of Potemkin Corporation's finance committee, as well as president of Swink & Company, investment bankers. Swink disagrees with Mr. Potemkin and urges Belcher to give careful consideration to the common stock. Swink argues, first, that the company's sales have experienced some sharp downturns in the past and that similar downturns in the future would endanger the viability of the firm. As Table 23.3 shows, sales declined sharply on three occasions: in 1964, when the company was involved in a long, drawn-out labor dispute; in 1967, when housing starts were severely depressed because of the tight money situation that existed during that year; and in 1969, when a fire closed down much of the company's manufacturing facilities for a substantial part of the year. Swink has pointed out to Belcher that the danger of a major fire in the firm's foundries is still present and that

Table 23.3

POTEMKIN CORPORATION
(in millions)

Year	Sales	Profit after Taxes	Dividends per share	Earnings per Share	Price of Stock
1971	$300	$31	$1.00	$3.85	$45
1970	270	25	1.00	3.12	44
1969	160	(5)	—	(.62)	31
1968	220	21	1.00	2.63	39
1967	160	7	1.00	.88	31
1966	189	18	.50	2.25	33
1965	175	17	.50	2.12	30
1964	97	(6)	—	(.75)	19
1963	152	14	.50	1.75	25
1962	140	13	.50	1.63	24

the major unions with which the industry deals are among the most militant in the entire United States.

Swink also disagrees with Potemkin with regard to the terms of the bond agreement. He observes that the dividend provision might require the company to forego paying cash dividends in any one year and that the combined cash drain on the firm, resulting from the required payment of interest plus the sinking fund, would be very serious in the event of a severe drop in sales. He also notes that the interest rate on the bonds would be 8 percent, which is high by historic standards, and that the company cannot call the bonds for 10 years, even if interest rates decline substantially from present levels.

Swink also points out one final factor to Belcher. The company's stock is currently traded over the counter, although the management group would like to obtain a New York Stock Exchange listing. When the company made a tentative application for listing on the Big Board it was denied on the grounds that (1) a large percentage of the stock is owned by management and members of the Potemkin family, so the floating supply would not be sufficient to meet New York Stock Exchange requirements and (2) the floating supply of stock does not have the broad geographic distribution required by the New York Stock Exchange. Swink emphasizes that if stock is sold through investment bankers, the distribution will be sufficiently broad and the number of shares outstanding sufficiently large to qualify the Potemkin Corporation for Big Board listing.

Belcher himself wonders if the preferred stock alternative might not overcome Mr. Potemkin's objections to common stock and Swink's objections to bonds and, thus, represent the best financing choice.

Questions

1. Assuming that the new funds earn the same rate of return currently being earned on the firm's assets (earnings before interest and taxes/total assets), what would earnings per share be under each of the three financing methods? (Assume that the new outside funds are employed during the whole year 1972, but that retained earnings for 1972 are not employed until 1973.)

2. Calculate the debt ratio at year-end 1972 under each of the financing alternatives. Assume 1972 current liabilities remain at the $45 million level and that additions to retained earnings for 1972 total $25 million. Compare Potemkin Corporation's figures with industry averages as given in Table 23.4.

3. Calculate the before-tax interest earned coverage for the year 1972 under each of the financing alternatives.

Table   23.4

POTEMKIN CORPORATION
PLUMBING EQUIPMENT INDUSTRY RATIOS

Debt/total assets[a]	35%
Times interest earned	10 times
Times burden covered	8 times
Profit after taxes/sales	6%
Profit after tax/total assets	8%
Profit after tax/net worth	12%
Price/earnings	14 times

[a] As the industry average ratio is calculated, debt does *not* include preferred stock.

4. Calculate the before-tax times burden covered (interest charges plus sinking fund requirements) under each of the three alternatives for the year 1972.
5. Assume that after the new capital is raised, fixed charges increase to $30 million and the ratio of variable cost to sales is 70 percent. How much would sales have to drop before the equity financing would be preferable to debt in terms of EPS?
6. What method of financing should Belcher recommend to the board? Fully justify your recommendation.

Computron, Inc.

(Stocks versus Bonds)

Ammex Corporation, a leading producer of magnetic sound equipment as well as television cameras and related materials, had invested approximately $10 million in research and development on computer products, including principally tape drives and high-speed printer equipment. After having spent the funds to develop the equipment, Ammex began to doubt the wisdom of entering into this highly competitive field. At the same time, growth in its traditional product lines was extremely high, and the company was experiencing difficulty in obtaining sufficient funds to support this growth. Because of these developments, Ammex decided, in 1965, to spin off its infant computer equipment manufacturing division, and as a result Computron, Inc., was founded.

Bruce Gray, Director of Ammex's Computer Division, had more faith in the new product designs than did the corporate management of Ammex, so Gray, with the support of the New York investment banking firm of Sherrill, Hampton and Company, obtained $10 million to purchase all of Ammex's rights to the new equipment and to establish a manufacturing facility. Operations commenced in the spring of 1965; during the remainder of that year sales totaled $2.0 million, while an operating loss of $500,000 was incurred. Sales increased to $6.1 million in 1966, and the operating loss was reduced. Thereafter, the company

117

operated in the black, with sales and profits growing to $47.9 million and $5.0 million, respectively, by 1971 (see Tables 24.1, 24.2, and 24.3). The price of the company's stock, which was traded over the counter from 1965 through 1969, when it was listed on the American Stock Exchange, is currently $34 a share, and it earned 45 cents a share during 1971.

The company has more than borne out Bruce Gray's expectations, and continued improvements in the product line, plus the development of a new data receiving and transmission unit suitable for sending data

Table   24.1

COMPUTRON, INC.
DECEMBER 31, 1971
(in millions)

Current assets	$24
Fixed assets	38
Total	$62
Current liabilities (accruals and accounts payable)	$ 9
Long-term debt (7.5%)	30
Common stock ($1 par)	11
Retained earnings	12
Total liabilities and net worth	$62

Table   24.2

COMPUTRON, INC.
YEAR ENDED DECEMBER 31, 1971
(in millions)

Sales	$47.9
Cost of goods sold[a]	33.2
Gross profit	$14.7
General and administrative expenses	2.1
Earnings before interest	$12.6
Interest charges	2.3
Earnings before taxes	$10.3
Taxes (52% marginal rate)	5.4
Net income	$ 4.9
Dividends	0.0
Addition to retained earnings	$ 4.9

[a] Includes depreciation charges of $5 million.

Table 24.3

COMPUTRON, INC.
(in millions)

Year	Sales	Profit after Taxes	Earnings per Share	Price of Stock
1971	$47.9	$4.9	$.45	$34
1970	38.6	3.5	.32	19
1969	27.5	2.1	.19	9½
1968	20.3	1.3	.12	6
1967	12.0	.7	.06	2½
1966	6.1	(.1)	(.1)	1½
1965	2.0	(.5)	—	1

through telephone lines, suggest that the company's growth trend in sales and profits will be continued. Thus far, Computron has met its financial requirements through retained earnings and long-term bank loans. Because of a shortage of funds, however, Gray's primary bank, the Bank of North America, has advised the company that its present $20 million line of credit cannot be increased. Therefore, the approximately $10 million (over and above funds available from retained earnings) needed to finance the projected assets expansion for 1972 must be obtained from sources other than the bank.

Neko Colvins, Financial Vice President, has decided that the three alternatives available to the company are sale of common stock, sale of preferred stock, or sale of a long-term bond issue that would be purchased by the Pacific Northwest Mutual Life Insurance Company. The terms under which each of these sources of funds would be made available, as reported to Colvins by Sherill, Hampton and Company, are as follows:

1. Common stock could be sold to net the company approximately $30 a share. Since the current price of the stock is approximately $34, this represents a brokerage cost of $4 a share.
2. The company could sell preferred stock, par value $100, that would pay a $10 annual dividend. The stock would be sold to net the company $95 a share; that is, an underwriting cost of $5 a share would be incurred. The preferred stock would not be callable for five years, after which it could be called at a price of $110 a share. No sinking fund would be used.
3. The company could sell $10 million of 15-year notes to the Pacific Northwest Mutual Life Insurance Company. The notes would be fully amortized over 15 years and would bear interest at a rate of 9 percent. The key provisions in the loan agreement would require (a) that the company maintain a current ratio of at least

2.5 to 1, (b) that cash dividends on common stock be paid only out of earnings generated after the loan agreement was signed, and (c) that the company would engage in no additional long-term debt financing without the agreement of the Pacific Northwest Mutual Life Insurance Company. The notes are callable, but at a call premium of 15 percent.

When the senior officers met to discuss these three possibilities, Gordon MacLeod, Executive Vice President, spoke up in favor of the common stock financing. MacLeod pointed out that the company enjoys a very high price-earnings ratio and that its capital structure is already over-loaded with debt relative to other firms in the industry. (See Table 24.4.)

Bruce Gray, however, questioned the use of common stock at this time. Observing that the company's sales and profit projections suggest that earnings will continue to increase at a substantial rate over the course of the next several years—indeed, if certain new developments now in the research and development stage bear fruit, the actual rate of increase could be increased significantly—he objected to "sharing this growth with new stockholders." In a hurried calculation, Gray projected that earnings could be as high as $2 a share by 1975. Assuming that the price-earnings ratio stays at its current level, this would mean that the company's stock would be selling for approximately $151 a share. Gray stated emphatically that he dislikes the idea of selling stock worth $151 a share for only $30 per share.

Arkel Erb, Sales Manager, cautioned Gray that he has information, which may or may not be correct, that a major computer manufacturer which purchases approximately 50 percent of Computron's output plans to start manufacturing these components itself. If this event actually occurs, Erb foresees that the firm's sales and profits will suffer drastically, at least until other markets can be developed to take up the slack.

Table   24.4

INDUSTRY RATIOS
COMPUTER EQUIPMENT MANUFACTURERS
($50–$70 MILLION ASSETS)

Debt/total assets[a]	40%
Times interest earned	12 times
Times burden covered	7 times
Profit after taxes/sales	10%
Profit after tax/total assets	10%
Profit after tax/net worth	17%
Price/earnings	40 times

[a] Preferred stock is not included in debt.

James Powell, Vice President, Production, backed up MacLeod's position and, in addition, indicated that costs of establishing production of the new data receiving and transmitting units might be higher than anticipated and, therefore, cause profits to temporarily drop below the anticipated levels. Because of these uncertainties, both Erb and Powell recommended the common stock alternative.

Colvins himself voiced the opinion that, as a compromise, perhaps the company should adopt the preferred stock alternative. Gray, Powell, and Erb all thought this suggestion was worth looking into, but after the meeting was over Colvins had some questions of his own about the proposal. His primary concern was that the after-tax cost of preferred stock is substantially higher than the after-tax cost of debt.

Questions

1. Assuming that the new funds earn the same rate of return currently earned on the firm's assets (earnings before interest and taxes/total assets), what would earnings per share be under each of the three financing methods? (Assume also that the new outside funds are employed during the whole year 1972 but that 1972 additions to retained earnings are not employed until 1973.)
2. Calculate the debt ratio, at year-end 1972, under each of the financing alternatives. Assume 1972 current liabilities remain at the $9 million level and that retained earnings, as shown on the balance sheet for the year 1972, are $20 million. (Notice that the assumed increase in Retained Earnings for this question is $8 million, whereas the earnings calculated in (1) were less than this amount. This change is made to simplify calculations.)
3. Calculate the before-tax times interest earned coverage for the year 1972 under each of the financing alternatives.
4. Calculate the before-tax times burden covered (interest charges plus loan amortization, or sinking fund, requirements) under each of the three alternatives for the year 1972.
5. Assuming that annual fixed costs will rise to $8 million after the new capital is acquired, and the ratio of variable costs to sales is 60 percent, how much must sales increase before bond financing becomes preferable to equity in terms of EPS?
6. What method of financing should Colvins recommend to the board?

Picwick's Department Store

(Sale and Leaseback)

Ed McKinnon, Financial Vice President of Picwick's Department Store, has just learned that a group of real estate developers is planning a major new residential and industrial subdivision in the northeast section of his city, and that they plan to build a large shopping center to service both the expected and present northeast area residents. The developers are anxious to have a major department store in the shopping center, and they have offered Picwick's a chance to open a new facility there. If Picwick's does not exercise this option to branch into the new center, the developers plan to hold discussions with several national department stores, including Gimbels, Marshall Field, and Macy's. McKinnon is quite certain that, given the expansionist mood in the department store industry, one of the national chains will move into the new shopping center if Picwick's does not.

Reviewing statistics on sales and profits for his company over the past 12 years (Table 25.1), McKinnon notes that sales increased by roughly 5 percent per year from 1960 to 1966, while profits increased similarly. In late 1966, however, a national department store chain opened a branch in a major new westside shopping center. As population on the west side of town grew, and as the new store gained experience in determining the types of goods desired, completed its personnel training program, and began to obtain the full impact of a heavy advertising budget, it com-

Table 25.1

PICWICK'S DEPARTMENT STORE

Year	Sales	Net Profit after Taxes[a]
1960	$23,500,000	$536,000
1961	24,700,000	556,000
1962	25,400,000	588,000
1963	26,600,000	609,000
1964	27,500,000	640,000
1965	28,900,000	672,000
1966	30,200,000	702,000
1967	30,800,000	685,000
1968	31,000,000	602,000
1969	30,600,000	540,000
1970	30,100,000	450,000
1971	30,300,000	460,000

[a] Tax rate = 50 percent.

NOTE: Depreciation charges during the period shown were $125,000 a year for furniture, fixtures, and equipment and $275,000 a year for the buildings.

pletely arrested Picwick's growth. Between 1968 and 1970, it caused an actual decline in Picwick's sales, and an even sharper decline in profits. By 1971, however, population growth in the community was sufficient to offset the impact of the new store, and Picwick's had a small increase in both sales and profits.

Although the new development is still several years away, if Picwick's does launch a new store, McKinnon must make plans for financing the venture. The recent trend in sales and profits will not help, and the balance sheet (Table 25.2) for 1970 also presents some problems. Picwick's debt ratio, at 50.7 percent versus 61.4 percent for the average department store, is good, but the company's liquidity position is quite weak. McKinnon calculates his own current ratio at 1.3 versus an industry average of 2.5.

As he sees it, Picwick's profitability can be increased to its pre-1967 level if the new store is inaugurated. The downtown facility is already making a comeback, and the new store, which would be opened in about 1975, would be very well situated. Further, the new facility should not make a material inroad on sales of the downtown store, as population growth in the area should be sufficient to provide an adequate market for both of these facilities, as well as for the west side competitor.

The problem is Picwick's liquidity position. With a current ratio of only 1.3 to 1, the bank is unwilling to extend any additional credit. Because of this, McKinnon has been unable to keep his accounts payable current. Of the $4.9 million accounts payable as of December 31, 1970, approxi-

Table 25.2

PICWICK'S DEPARTMENT STORE
Year Ended December 31, 1970

Cash	$ 400,000
Accounts receivable	2,100,000
Inventories	5,600,000
Total current assets	$ 8,100,000
Furniture, fixtures, and equipment	1,500,000
(cost $3,000,000 less depreciation, $1,500,000)	
Buildings (Cost $7,500,000 less depreciation, $3,300,000)	4,200,000
Land	400,000
Total assets	$14,200,000
Accounts payable	$ 4,900,000
Notes payable	1,300,000
Total current liabilities	$ 6,200,000
Mortgage on land and buildings (6%)	1,000,000
Net worth	7,000,000
Total liabilities and net worth	$14,200,000

	Picwick's	Industry Average
Current ratio	1.3 times	2.5 times
Debt ratio	50.7%	61.4%

mately $3 million are past due. Picwick's has, of course, been unable to take any trade discounts, and its reputation as a slow payer is causing it some difficulty. McKinnon is quite sure that this reputation will present a serious problem when he attempts to raise funds to finance the new store. Accordingly, he must clear up the liquidity problem before he attempts to obtain new financing.

In his discussions with a local investment banker, McKinnon has learned that he could increase the mortgage on the company's present fixed assets to $4 million. This would require paying off the present 6 percent mortgage loan and taking on a new $4 million loan at 8 percent. Alternatively, Picwick's could sell the land and buildings (but retain title to the furniture, fixtures, and equipment) to a wealthy industrialist for the approximate market value of these fixed assets—$4 million. Picwick's would immediately lease the assets back on a 20-year lease for a rental of $377,500 per year. A quick calculation of the interest rate implicit in the lease payment told McKinnon that the rate built into the lease was only 7 percent. When he asked the investment banker why Picwick's would be able to obtain a 7 percent lease in a period when mortgage money was going for 8 percent, the banker informed him that the industrialist, being in a 70 percent tax bracket and able to depreciate the building against his own income, thought that tax advantages to him would be sufficient to permit him to make the lease on a 7 percent basis.

McKinnon also noted that, in the event of the sale and leaseback, the stated purchase price that the industrialist would pay Picwick's would be $500,000 for the land and $3,500,000 for the buildings. These sums approximate the existing market values of the two components.

Questions

1. How much will Picwick's net if it (a) takes the sale and lease-back or (b) increases the size of its mortgage? Assume Picwick's has no other capital gains or losses, either in this year or carried forward.
2. Will either, or both, of the two financing plans permit Picwick's to become current in its accounts payable?
3. The lease payments on a $4 million sale and leaseback will amount to $377,500 per year for 20 years (all of this is a tax deduction). The payments of a 20-year mortgage will amount to $407,000 per year, consisting of $320,000 interest and $87,000 repayment of principal for the first year. Calculate the nominal rate of interest, disregarding capital gains or losses, on each of these two instruments.
4. The investment banker gave the treatment of depreciation by the investor who would make the sale and leaseback as the reason for the differential in effective interest rates in 3. Can you think of any additional factor that might account for the difference in the two rates?
5. (a) If the lease had been in effect during 1971, what would Picwick's 1971 profit have been? (b) What would the profit have been had the larger mortgage loan been in effect? (HINT: Work backward to build up *pro forma* earnings before interest and taxes for 1971, then use this figure to answer the question.)
6. Which of the two alternative financing methods, if either, should Ed McKinnon recommend to his store's board of directors?

Zircon Steel Corporation

(Lease versus Loan)

As part of its modernization and cost-reduction program, Zircon Steel plans to install a new computer system to control the steel manufacturing process in its Pittsburgh plant on January 1, 1971. Benefits from using the new system, which include savings in labor and raw materials as well as improved quality, are large enough to make the new control system well worthwhile. In the capital budgeting analysis made prior to the decision to go ahead with the new system, the internal rate of return on the project was found to be approximately 30 percent versus the firm's average cost of capital of 10 percent. (The company uses a cost of capital of 8 percent for relatively low-risk projects and 12 percent for those with above average risk. This particular project is estimated to carry an average degree of risk.)

The computer system has an invoice price of $140,000, delivered and installed. This sum can be borrowed from the bank on a five-year amortized loan at an 8 percent interest rate. The computer manufacturer will maintain and service the machine, in the event that it is purchased, for a charge of $8,750 per year. Zircon Steel uses the sum-of-the-years digits method for calculating depreciation, and it is in the 50 percent tax bracket.

The manufacturer has offered to lease the computer to Zircon Steel for $38,000 a year on a five-year lease. The computer actually has an expected life of approximately 10 years, at which time it should be worthless. However, it has an estimated resale value of $38,000 (the book value) at the end of 1975, the fifth year, but Zircon plans to modernize the Pittsburgh facility in early 1976. Since a continuous casting process will be installed, and since the new system will have its own control devices, Zircon is not interested in leasing the equipment for more than five years. The lease includes a service contract under which the manufacturer will maintain the equipment in good working order.

William Knowles, Financial Vice President, must make a recommendation to the finance committee on whether to borrow money from the bank at 8 percent and purchase the equipment outright or to lease the equipment for five years. Zircon Steel's standard method of making lease versus purchase decisions is to calculate the net present value cost of lease payments versus the present value of total charges if the equipment is purchased. However, in a recent meeting of the finance committee, in which a decision similar to the one presently being considered came up, there was a heated discussion as to the appropriate discount rate to use in determining the present value costs of leasing and of purchasing. The following points of view were expressed:

1. The discount rate should be the firm's average cost of capital. A lease versus purchase decision is, in effect, a capital budgeting decision, and, as such, it should be evaluated at the firm's cost of capital. In other words, one method or the other will provide a cost saving in any given year. The dollars saved by the most advantageous method will be invested to yield the firm's average cost of capital; therefore, the average cost of capital is the appropriate discount rate for use in evaluating leasing versus purchasing.

2. The cash flows generated in a lease versus purchase situation are more certain than are the cash flows generated from the firm's average projects. Therefore, these cash flows should be discounted at a low risk rate. At the present time, the firm's cost of debt reflects the lowest risk rate to Zircon Steel; therefore, 8 percent should be used as the discount rate in the lease versus purchase decision.

3. A variant of the second suggestion calls for using an after-tax riskless rate of return. In other words, with an 8 percent interest rate to the company, the appropriate discount rate for use in the lease versus purchase decision would be 4 percent with a 50 percent tax rate.

In the last lease versus purchase decision, the average cost of capital —10 percent—was used, but on reflection Knowles doubts the validity of this procedure. He is inclined toward the third alternative presented, but he wonders if it would be appropriate to use a low-risk discount rate for evaluating all cash flows in the analysis. In particular, Knowles is concerned over the risk on the differential cash flows of the lease-loan decision as compared to the risk of the expected salvage value. While the firm is almost certain of the flows required by the lease or loan, the salvage value is relatively uncertain, having a distribution of possible outcomes that makes its risk comparable to the risk of the average projects undertaken by the firm.

Questions

1. Set up a worksheet and calculate the comparative cost of leasing versus buying the new computer. (NOTE: The computer must be depreciated over 10 years, so for purposes of this case, the first year's depreciation is $10/55 \times \$140,000 = \$25,000$, and so on.)
2. Justify the discount rate or rates that you used in the calculating process.
3. How would it affect your analysis if Zircon Steel used straight-line depreciation rather than the sum-of-the-years digits method? (Do not make a calculation; just indicate the direction of the effect.)
4. Assume Zircon leased the equipment and that the value of the leased property ($140,000) was a substantial sum of money in relation to Zircon Steel's total assets. What problems might this cause for outside financial analysts, and how might such analysts solve the problem?
5. Should Zircon lease or buy?
6. In some instances, it might be possible for a leasing company to offer a contract with a cost *less than* the debt cost that the firm would encounter if it were to attempt to finance the purchase. If the equipment represented a significant addition to the firm's assets, could this affect its overall cost of capital?

Case / 27

Bremen Aircraft, Inc.

(Warrants and Convertibles)

Sewell McKesson, Financial Vice President of Bremen Aircraft, Inc., is reviewing a number of alternative financing proposals that he has just received from McCall, Thomas & Company, investment bankers. Bremen Aircraft's board of directors will hold a special meeting in three days to decide how to finance a major expansion program, and McKesson must evaluate the alternatives and make a recommendation to the board at that time.

Bremen Aircraft Company is one of the largest manufacturers of small, nonmilitary aircraft in the nation. The company was founded in 1923, grew very slowly during the 1920s and 1930s, expanded rapidly during World War II as a producer of light aircraft used for artillery-spotting purposes, and has experienced steady and profitable growth since the termination of the war. In 1969, the company's research and development staff completed plans for a vertical take-off and landing aircraft suitable for use as an ambulance capable of operating on intercity highways. A model of the ambulance aircraft was developed in 1970, and by the end of 1971 a working prototype had been test flown and demonstrated to state and local authorities.

The company has received firm offers for 50 of the new planes from several key states. Officials of these states have indicated that if the planes work out in actual operation as well as anticipated they will purchase approximately 500 more. Most of the remaining states, as well as several agencies of the federal government, have also expressed a keen interest in the planes and are awaiting the results of the actual usage. Bremen Aircraft has not contacted any foreign governments, but officials of the company are convinced that, assuming the operating results are satisfactory, substantial foreign orders will also be forthcoming.

Bremen Aircraft's production facilities are operating at close to capacity, so the ambulance aircraft cannot be produced on a large scale without a substantial expansion. The cost of the new facilities, and the working capital necessary to operate these facilities, has been estimated at $15 million. All of these funds must be generated externally.

Bremen Aircraft's investment bankers have indicated that the $15 million can be raised by any one of several methods which they have submitted to the company. These proposals are shown in Table 27.1. Although the bankers originally recommended either common stock, non-convertible debentures, or the 5½ percent bonds convertible into common stock at $55 a share, at McKesson's request they reluctantly supplied him with additional information on an alternative convertible issue and also on bonds with warrants (alternatives 4 and 5 in Table 27.1). In their conversations with him, the investment bankers have indicated to McKesson that investors today appear to like convertibles with a conversion price set relatively close to the present market price of the stock, and that they seem to prefer convertibles rather than bonds with warrants.

In discussions between the accounting and finance departments, there was some question about the effect that either warrants or convertibles would have on the firm's financial reports, particularly on reported earnings immediately after conversion. McKesson believes that the current price of the stock reflects the higher growth in earnings over the last few years, and is worried that the dilution occurring after conversion or exercise might adversely affect price.

Table 27.1

BREMEN AIRCRAFT COMPANY
FINANCING ALTERNATIVES[a]

1. Common stock to net $50 a share.
2. Nonconvertible debentures, effective cost 7 percent.
3. Convertible debentures, 5½ percent, convertible at $55 a share after 1975.
4. Convertible debentures, 6½ percent, convertible at $70 a share after 1975.
5. Bonds with warrants, 5½ percent; each bond has 15 warrants, entitling the holder to buy one share at $55 after 1975.

[a] Flotation costs would be slightly higher for common stock, convertibles, and bonds with warrants than for nonconvertible debentures.

Thus far the company has been able to obtain all of its equity capital requirements by retaining earnings, and its long-term debt has been acquired in the form of private placements from insurance companies. The insurance companies with which McKesson has done business in the past have indicated that they would be willing to lend Bremen Aircraft additional capital at the present time at an interest rate of 7 to 7½ percent, but that the company's debt ratio is beginning to get out of line (see Table 27.2). The insurance company loan officers have suggested

Table 27.2

BREMEN AIRCRAFT COMPANY
DECEMBER 31, 1971
 (in millions)

		Current liabilities	$16.7
		(accounts payable)	
Current assets	$38.0	Long-term debt (7%)	27.0
Fixed assets	47.2	Net worth	41.5
	$85.2		$85.2

that they would be much happier to see Bremen Aircraft obtain some additional equity capital to bring the debt ratio more into line with that of other manufacturing companies. Since in the future McKesson would like to borrow again from these insurance companies, he is anxious to maintain his company's reputation as a good credit risk.

The price of Bremen's stock did not increase as rapidly in the late 1960s as it did in the earlier part of the decade. However, McKesson is quite happy with the stock's annual growth from 1966 to 1971 and predicts that this rate of increase will continue into the 1970s. Other projected financial statistics are shown in Table 27.3.

The current market price of Bremen's stock is $50 per share, and management estimates that the 1975 year-end price of the stock has the following probability distribution of expected values:

Price	Probability
$65.00	.15
70.00	.20
75.00	.30
80.00	.20
85.00	.15

Table 27.3

BREMEN AIRCRAFT COMPANY

Year	Sales (millions)	Earnings before Interest and Taxes (millions)	Net Profit[b] (millions)	Earnings per Share[c]	Dividends per Share	Addition to Retained Earnings (millions)[a]
1961	$ 35.2	$ 6.7	$2.4	$ .95	$ .25	$1.8
1962	42.1	6.8	2.5	.99	.25	1.9
1963	49.6	7.3	2.7	1.07	.25	2.1
1964	56.5	7.5	2.9	1.15	.50	1.6
1965	58.7	8.7	3.3	1.31	.50	2.0
1966	63.3	9.7	3.9	1.55	.60	2.4
1967	69.5	10.8	4.4	1.74	.60	2.9
1968	73.8	11.8	4.9	1.94	.60	3.4
1969	85.2	12.5	5.3	2.10	.75	3.4
1970	91.8	13.3	5.7	2.26	.75	3.8
1971	102.0	14.5	6.3	2.50	1.00	3.8
1972[a]	112.2					4.2
1973[a]	123.4					4.7
1974[a]	135.7					5.1
1975[a]	149.3					5.7
1976[a]	164.2					6.2

[a] Projections, assuming the $15 million investment is made.
[b] Assumes a 50 percent tax rate.
[c] 2,500,000 shares outstanding at year-end 1971.
[d] These figures would vary depending upon the financing method used, but the differences are not large enough to affect seriously the required calculations.

Questions

1. Bremen Aircraft's rate of return before taxes on total assets (earnings before interest and taxes/total assets) was 17 percent in 1971. Assuming that this rate will be maintained in the future, calculate the approximate earnings per share and debt ratios under each of the five alternatives for 1972 and 1976. Assume that 1972 additions to retained earnings are not employed until 1973, and 1976 additions are not employed until 1977. In addition, McKesson believes that if the year-end price of the stock is above the conversion price or option price, then conversion will take place or warrants will be exercised. Assume that (a) the entire conversion takes place at the beginning of the year, (b) no interest is paid on the converted debt after conversion, (c) EPS is based on all shares outstanding at year-end, including shares issued through conversion at the beginning of the year. Whenever possible, use projections from Table 27.3 and assume that current liabilities will spontaneously increase by $1.3 million with the higher 1972 sales level, and will reach a level of $26 million in 1976. To simplify computation, some of the figures have already been indicated in Table 27.4.

Table 27.4

		Financing Method				
		1	*2*	*3*	*4*	*5*
EPS	1972	$2.74	—	$2.90	—	$2.90
	1976	—	$3.80	—	$3.69	—
Shares Outstanding	1976	2.8m	—	2.773m	—	—
Debt Ratio	1972	—	56.8	—	56.8	56.8
(Percent)	1976	39.1	—	39.1	—	—

As an example of how the calculations might be made, for the third financing proposal (5½ percent convertibles), the first figure required is 1972 EBIT, which may be estimated as 17 percent of the asset level at the beginning of the year. This projected level is the 1971 level, plus the new financing, plus the increase in current liabilities:

$$\text{EBIT} = (\$85.2m + \$15.0m + \$1.3m)\,(.17) = \$17.25m$$

The price of the stock at the end of 1971 was $50, and conversion would not take place. Thus, there would be 2.5 million shares outstanding. EPS would be calculated as:

EBIT		$17,250,000
Interest on 1971 debt	$1,890,000	
Interest on new debt	825,000	2,715,000
EBT		$14,535,000
Taxes (50%)		7,267,500
Earnings		$ 7,267,500
EPS (2.5m shares out)		$2.90

Debt ratio under this method for 1972 would be computed by taking the total asset figure given above ($101.5 million), adding the $4.2 million in retained earnings from 1972 (not considered productive during 1972) for a total of $105.7 million. Debt will equal the 1971 level ($43.7 million), plus the new debt ($15 million), plus the new current liabilities ($1.3 million), a total of $60 million. The debt ratio is therefore equal to $60/$105.7=56.8 percent.

2. What would the effect be on existing stockholders and holders of the convertible debentures or warrants if Bremen Aircraft changes its dividend policy as follows: (a) increases its dividend payout to 100 percent; (b) decreases its dividend payout to zero percent?

3. The investment bankers' preliminary proposal did not mention certain items that may or may not be in the final contracts. McKesson knows, however, that these points will come up when he enters into a more detailed discussion with the bankers. What should he recommend with regard to each of the following points, keeping in mind that he must be "reasonable"? (a) Stepped-up conversion prices and warrant exercise prices. For example, the conversion or exercise price could be increased by $5 a share after some period, say five years. (b) A call feature and, if it is used, a call price. (c) A sinking fund. (d) Provisions for stock dividends or stock splits.

4. If the Bremen Aircraft management had decided on the use of some type of convertible financing (convertibles or bonds with warrants) but was concerned with the exact timing of the conversion, which of the two methods would be preferable?

5. Evaluate McKesson's comments on the possible effects of dilution on stock price. How might the company mitigate the effects of the future dilution of earnings?

6. What method of financing should McKesson recommend?

Pacific Oil Company

(Convertibles)

Jane Weber, age 38, has just had a shattering experience. On the evening of Friday, November 12, 1971, she calculated her net worth to be $148,200. With the exception of $5,000 equity in her home, her investments were in relatively safe—she thought—convertible bonds. But on Monday, November 15, after losing $58,000 in one day, Miss Weber is not so sure about the safety of her portfolio.

Miss Weber's market holdings are shown in Table 28.1. On that particular Friday, she owned the convertible debentures of three companies, with the bulk of her holdings in Pacific Oil. Her original cost was $175,000, but the market value of the convertibles had increased to $383,000 by November 13th. When the market value of securities increases, one may borrow additional funds to purchase new securities. Since she had followed this practice, by the Friday in question the total borrowing in her margin account was $250,000.[1] Her net ownership was thus $143,200, up from an original investment of about $50,000.

---

[1] The Federal Reserve Board imposes limits on borrowing against certain listed securities. Prior to 1969, there were no limits on convertibles such as those on common stocks. After 1969, margin requirements were imposed on the bonds of certain corporations. None of the companies whose convertibles Miss Weber held fell in this category, and her broker permitted her to borrow up to 70 percent of the market value of her holdings.

Table 28.1

JANE WEBER'S PORTFOLIO

November 13, 1971

	Original Cost	*Present Value*	*Margin Borrowing*[a]	*Net Worth*
Pacific Oil	$145,000	$290,000		
Southeast Airlines	10,000	85,000		
U.S. Motors	20,000	18,200		
	$175,000	$393,200	$250,000	$143,200

November 16, 1971

Pacific Oil	$145,000	$232,000		
Southeast Airlines	10,000	85,000		
U.S. Motors	20,000	18,200		
	$175,000	$335,200	$250,000	$ 85,200

[a] Borrowed against the total value of the portfolio, not against individual securities

Miss Weber is a vice president and loan officer of First California Bank, the principal bank of Pacific Oil. Although Miss Weber does not handle the Pacific Oil account, she had studied Pacific's history, present situation, and prospects carefully, and she had gone over her review with the loan officer who does manage the account. On the basis of this analysis, when Miss Weber received a substantial inheritance eight months earlier, she invested it in the Pacific Oil convertibles. Miss Weber felt that while the company's common stock was relatively risky, the convertibles offered an assured 4½ percent yield, with the possibility of a substantial capital gain.

Shortly after Miss Weber purchased the Pacific bonds the company announced a substantial oil strike in the Algerian desert. As a result, the price of the stock doubled, moving from $20 to $40, and the convertible bonds also doubled in price. Then, two weeks ago, Pacific Oil announced that it was making an offer to the shareholders of Marin County Land Company to buy Marin County stock at $80 a share. Since Marin County Land was selling at approximately $60 a share on the New York Stock Exchange at the time of the offer, there was every reason to believe that most Marin County stockholders would tender their stock to Pacific Oil.

Miss Weber learned from the loan officer handling the Pacific Oil account that a group of banks, including her own, had agreed to lend Pacific Oil the approximately $120 million necessary to complete the transaction. The banks had stipulated, however, that Pacific Oil must call its convertible bond issue to bring the debt ratio down to an acceptable level prior to finalizing the new loan. The banks, obviously, were afraid that some unforeseen event would occur that might cause the price of Pacific Oil's stock to decline, and they were anxious to see the convertibles converted into common stock before making the substantial new loan.

Although Miss Weber had known all of the above facts the previous week, she had decided not to sell her Pacific Oil convertibles, reasoning that, because Marin County Land was actually worth substantially more than the $80 per share offered by Pacific, the proposed merger, when it took place, would cause Pacific's common stock to rise still more, pulling the price of the convertible bonds up with it.

On Monday, November 15th, Pacific called the convertible debenture issue; the price of the debentures fell from $2,000 per bond to $1,600 per bond; and Miss Weber's net worth dropped from $143,200 to $85,200, a loss of $58,000. Being rather upset, Miss Weber decided to reexamine her entire portfolio. As a first step, she compiled the information shown in Table 28.2 for each of the three convertible issues.

Table 28.2

INFORMATION ON PORTFOLIO

Pacific Oil

On February 17, 1970, bought at par 145 $1,000 bonds, 4½ percent, convertible into 40 shares of stock (conversion price: $25 per share). The bonds mature in 1999. Market price of stock at time of bond issue: $20 per share. On November 16, 1971, the market price of the stock was $40 and the market value of the bonds was $1,600. Pacific stock pays a $1 dividend.

Southeast Airlines

On December 16, 1968, bought at par 10 $1,000 bonds, 3½ percent, convertible into 20 shares of stock (conversion price: $50 per share). The bonds mature in 1995. Market price of stock at time of bond issue: $40 per share. On November 16, 1971, the market price of the stock was $400, and the market price of the bonds was $8,500. The stock pays a $10 dividend. Originally there were $15 million par value of convertibles outstanding. Now all except $600,-000 have been converted voluntarily. The conversion price rises to $60 on January 1, 1972, and to $70 on January 1, 1977.

U.S. Motors

On January 10, 1970, bought at par 20 $1,000 bonds, 6 percent, convertible into 50 shares of stock (conversion price: $20). Market price of stock at time of bond issue: $25 per share. On November 16, 1971, the market price of the stock was $10 per share. The stock pays no dividends, and the prospects for the stock are not good. The market price of the bonds, which mature in 1979, is $910, providing a yield to maturity (interest from 1971 through 1979, plus capital gain from $910 to par value of $1,000) of 7½ percent. U.S. Motors recently sold a $20 million issue of subordinated debentures (nonconvertible) to yield investors 7½ percent. These bonds have the same degree of risk of default as the convertibles.

Questions

1. Compare the November 16, 1971, market value of each convertible bond with its conversion value for all three convertible issues held by Miss Weber. What is the significance of these figures?
2. Compare current interest yields on the bonds with dividend yields on the related stocks for each of the convertible issues. Of what significance are these figures?
3. Evaluate Miss Weber's decision to hold the Pacific bonds in the face of the impending merger.
4. What should Miss Weber do with each of the three issues: hold the bonds, sell them at the current market price, or convert them into common stock? Fully justify your answers.

Part V

Working Capital Management

The New-Way Box Company

(Working Capital Policy)

The New-Way Box Company was formed in 1960 to manufacture a new type of wooden box used to pack fresh fruits and vegetables. The company has expanded rapidly since 1960, when its first plant, in California, was established. In 1965 the company placed two other plants on line, one in south Texas and one in southern Florida, and capacity has been increased annually at all three plants. Since New-Way produces different types of boxes for various products, its sales are not affected extensively by the seasonal patterns that are normally associated with agricultural crops.

New-Way's primary problem has been to increase production enough to meet the demand for its products. Although the company has been expanding rapidly, it has frequently lost sales because of insufficient production. Recognizing this problem, Peter Abbott, President and Chief Executive Officer, called a meeting of the top officers and interested directors to consider ways of increasing production. Those present at the meeting included Arthur S. Gordon, Vice President for Operations; Richard M. Paterson, Vice President for Finance and Accounting; and Wilbert J. Preston, Director and banker. Abbott began the discussion by describing the problem and by asking for suggestions from the participants.

Art Gordon led off the discussion by reporting that the sales department had indicated that it could sell over 2 million #16 boxes during the current grapefruit season in Texas, but that he must limit production to 1.2 million. This cutback is necessary in order to get the plant ready to produce #8 and #9 boxes, used to pack lettuce, celery, and other vegetables, prior to the start of their seasons. Production of #8's and #9's, in turn, will have to be curtailed before demand for them is fully satisfied to ready the production line for #12's, used for the tomato crop. This same situation, which has existed in the past, will continue in the future unless additional manufacturing equipment is installed.

Will Preston, the banker, agreed that it is important to obtain more equipment, but he indicated that the company will have difficulty obtaining additional long-term debt financing at the present time. New-Way's debt ratio is, in Preston's opinion, as high as long-term lenders will permit without charging a healthy risk premium on the new debt. Accordingly, he suggests that the proposed expansion be financed by a new issue of common stock.

The President, Peter Abbott, interrupted at this point, stating that a stock offering was probably out of the question. The present shareholders are not in a position to buy additional stock, and a sale to outsiders would raise serious control problems.

Dick Paterson, who has responsibility for financing and accounting, entered the discussion, stating, first, that he was not convinced that New-Way Company could not borrow additional long-term capital, but that if neither long-term debt nor common stock could be increased in sufficient quantities to purchase the needed equipment, the only avenues open for financing new equipment were leasing, short-term borrowing, increasing retained earnings, or reducing working capital. Restrictions in the company's long-term loan agreements made leasing difficult, and to increase retained earnings by cutting the dividend would worsen stockholder relations and increase the danger of control problems. Thus, Paterson stated, the best way to obtain funds for expanding plant capacity would be in the working capital area. Current liabilities might be increased, or current assets might be decreased, to generate the needed funds.

Mr. Preston interrupted, stating that there were definite limits on the company's ability to increase current liabilities and reduce current assets, and if these limits were exceeded, risk level would become excessive. There would be too high a probability of a default problem if the firm's liquidity position fell below a "safe" level.

Dick Paterson interjected that working capital management is a function of several relationships, including those between (1) current and fixed assets, (2) long- and short-term debt, and (3) total debt and total equity. Further, working capital policy is profoundly influenced by the willingness of stockholders and management to take risks. Paterson stated that New-Way's working capital policy was, in his opinion, quite conservative, and to support this contention, he presented Table 29.1, which he had constructed especially for the meeting. New-Way has more current assets, and consequently a higher current ratio, than the average firm in the industry. If the industry average is defined as "normal," New-Way is definitely conservative. Paterson concluded by stating that a shift to the industry average would make available a considerable amount of money which could be used to increase plant capacity.

Reflecting his banking background, Will Preston indicated an apprehensiveness about any change in working capital policy, then left the group to attend a meeting of his bank's board of directors. Peter Abbott asked if the ratio of sales to fixed assets, and of expenses to sales, as shown in section C of Table 29.1, would change if a new working capital policy was adopted. Art Gordon stated that these ratios could be maintained if fixed assets were not increased more than 30 percent above their present levels. He did not want to commit himself if the increase in fixed assets exceeded 30 percent.

It became clear to the group that more analysis would be required before a decision could be made. Three alternatives were identified: Policy C, under which the firm's current conservative policy would be maintained; Policy I, calling for a movement toward the industry average by reducing current assets to the industry average percentage, using the funds so generated to purchase fixed assets, but no change in liabilities or capital; and Policy A, an aggressive policy calling for decreasing current assets by 20 percent, increasing current liabilities by 20 percent, and using the funds obtained to purchase new fixed assets. Long-term debt and equity would be maintained at present levels under all three policies. New-Way can borrow short-term funds at $7\frac{1}{2}$ percent, long-term funds at 9 percent. Mr. Paterson was asked to prepare an analysis of these possibilities for the next meeting of the group, and it was agreed that the group would meet to discuss the alternatives in two weeks. It was further agreed that if a decision was reached to change the basic working capital policy, subsequent decisions would have to be made regarding the specific current asset components—cash, accounts receivable, marketable securities, and inventories—that would have to be changed. However, Paterson was asked to omit these considerations at the present time.

Questions

1. Prepare an exhibit that will illustrate the effects of the alternative policies on New-Way's financial position. Show each of the following items for each policy: (a) balance sheet, (b) income statement assuming the policy had been in effect for one year, and (c) the following ratios: current, total debt/assets, times interest earned,

Table 29.1

NEW-WAY BOX COMPANY
DATA ON ALTERNATIVE WORKING CAPITAL POLICIES
(All Dollars in Millions)

	Current Balance Sheet (12/31/72)		Industry Average Percentage
A. Balance Sheet			
Current Assets	$ 4.0	40%	36%
Net Fixed Assets	6.0	60	64%
Total Assets	$10.0	100%	100%
Current Liabilities (7½%)	$ 1.3	13%	13%
Long-Term Debt (9%)	4.0	40	40
Common Stock	4.7	47	47
	$10.0	100%	100%

B. Income Statement Data

Sales	$10.00
Operating Expenses	8.50
Earnings Before Interest and Taxes	$1.50
Interest	.46
Taxable Income	$ 1.04
Taxes (50%)	.52
Net Income	$ .52

C. Significant Ratios	New-Way	Industry
Sales/Fixed Assets	1.67X	1.60X
Current Ratio	3:1	2:77:1
Rate of Return on Equity	11.1%	10.21%
Expenses Other Than Interest and Taxes to Sales	85%	86%
Debt/Total Assets	53%	53%
Times Interest Earned	3.28X	3.22X

and rate of return on equity. In preparing the exhibit, hold constant common stock and long-term debt.

2. Compare the times interest earned and current ratios under the three alternative policies. What do you consider to be the primary factors that influence the relative riskiness of the alternative policies? Discuss their influence in the present case, quantifying the factors where possible, and indicating the type data needed to quantify the risks (and the feasibility of obtaining such data) where it is not given in the case.

3. Which policy should Paterson recommend at the next meeting? Explain your answer

4. The data given in the case indicate that the yield curve is upward sloping. (A "yield curve" is a graph showing the interest rate for a given debt instrument on the vertical axis and the years to maturity of the particular instrument on the horizontal axis.) (a) Do yield curves always slope upward? (b) How do expectations about future interest rates affect the shape of the yield curve? (c) If expectations are for no change in the general level of interest rates, what factors would probably impart an upward slope to the yield curve? (d) How would Mr. Paterson's personal feelings about future yield curves influence his feelings about New-Way's maturity-structure-of-debt aspects of working capital policy? (NOTE: Students not familiar with the structure of interest rates might wish to refer to J. Fred Weston and Eugene F. Brigham, *Managerial Finance*, 4th Ed., New York: Holt, Rinehart and Winston, Inc., 1972, Appendix to Chapter 25.)

Texas Land Company

(Disposal of Excess Working Capital)

Peter Dye, a partner in the management consulting firm of Prince, Allen and Hunt, is reviewing the recent financial statements of the Texas Land Company, one of his clients. Because of cyclical developments in one of Texas Land's major divisions, sales and profits have recently experienced a serious decline, and Dye's company has been retained to help Texas Land decide what action, if any, should be taken as a result of these developments.

The Texas Land Company was formed in the 1880s by a group of farmers and cattlemen who owned substantial acreages in east Texas. The original purpose of the company was to obtain greater economies of scale in clearing and developing land, purchasing livestock, and marketing the group's products. However, the nature of the company changed markedly in the 1920s when oil was discovered on the property. At that time the company was split into two divisions, one a land use division that concentrated on farming operations and the other an oil division that simply leased mineral rights to the company's oil to major oil companies. Within a very few years after the discovery of oil on the property, the oil division, while very small in terms of the number of people employed, was contributing about 80 percent of the firm's revenues and profits.

As the firm's original founders died, and as their estates were split up among their descendants, the stock gradually changed from being closely held to publicly owned, and in the late 1930s the stock was listed on the New York Stock Exchange. In spite of the broad ownership of the company, and in spite of the fact that its oil revenues made it one of the largest companies in the country, Texas Land was managed in a most unimaginative manner until the early 1950s. In 1952, the major stockholders concluded that the company was not using its assets in a sufficiently profitable manner, and Paul Byrnes, an individual with broad experience in the oil industry, was brought in as president and chief executive officer.

Byrnes' major decision was to use the cash flows generated by the Texas Land Company to acquire firms in other industries, principally manufacturers of farm equipment. This expansion program did increase sales and profits, but the manufacturing division, while not unprofitable, was not a notable success. In fact, because the problems experienced with the new companies in the manufacturing division proved to be so vexing, Texas Land suspended its acquisition program. Peter Dye, and most other sophisticated observers of the business scene, regarded Texas Land as a big, blundering company fortunate enough to hold title to some very valuable properties.

Sales in the farm equipment industry tend to be cyclical and move up or down depending on such factors as weather conditions, government price supports, conditions in export markets, and the like. Though 1968 was a good year for farmers and manufacturers of farm equipment, 1969 saw a down turn in sales and profits for farm equipment manufacturers, and 1970 was one of the poorest years since the end of World War II. As a result of these industry-wide trends, Texas Land Company's manufacturing division experienced a sharp decline in sales and earnings between 1968 and 1970. In fact, in 1970 the manufacturing division actually suffered a loss, but steady profits in the oil division were sufficient to enable the company to show an overall profit of $12 million.

As sales declined, accounts receivable also declined, and inventories were liquidated somewhat to reflect the lower level of sales. Although part of the funds generated by the reduction of accounts receivable and sales was invested in short-term marketable securities, Texas Land Company's cash balances in banks still increased substantially between 1968 and 1970. These trends are shown in Table 30.1. The declining volume of business caused a significant reduction in profits and earnings per share, which, in turn, caused a drop in the price of Texas Land's stock. These trends are shown in Table 30.2.

In his report to the directors, Peter Dye intends to make some recommendations for significant and fundamental changes in Texas Land's operations, which he believes will cause profits to rise substantially above the 1968 level within a few years. If the recommendations are followed, the funds currently in excess will be profitably employed in fixed assets.

Table   30.1

TEXAS LAND COMPANY
YEAR ENDED DECEMBER 31
(in millions)

	1968	1969	1970
Cash	$ 13.8	$ 20.8	$ 28.1
Marketable securities	—	13.9	28.2
Accounts receivable	55.0	41.6	35.2
Inventories	68.7	62.4	49.3
Total current assets	$137.5	$138.7	$140.8
Fixed assets	103.2	104.5	106.2
Total assets	$240.7	$243.2	$247.0
Total current liabilities	$ 43.9	$ 33.7	$ 34.4
Long-term debt (4%)	15.0	15.0	15.0
Common equity (stock plus surplus)	181.8	194.5	197.6
Total liabilities and net worth	$240.7	$243.2	$247.0

Table   30.2

TEXAS LAND COMPANY

	1968	1969	1970
Sales (millions)	$481.00	$453.00	$428.00
Profits (millions)	28.00	18.70	12.00
Dividends (millions)	6.00	6.00	8.90
Earnings per share	4.50	3.00	1.93
Dividends per share	0.96	0.96	1.43
Price of stock per share	90.00	60.00	45.00

However, the final report is not scheduled for completion for another six months, after which the directors will have to decide what to do and then take some action. All this will take about a year, and Dye believes that action should be taken immediately to reduce the excessive and unprofitable liquidity of the company. Therefore, he plans to submit a partial report containing suggestions for disposing of excess working capital. He lists the following alternatives for the consideration of Texas Land's directors:

1. The long-term debt could be retired. The insurance company that holds the bonds, which are due in 1995, is willing to permit the company to retire the bonds at the present time without penalty.
2. Some of the cash could be used to buy additional short-term mar-

ketable securities, such as Treasury bills, commercial paper, certificates of deposit, and the like. Treasury bills currently are yielding 7½ percent, while commercial paper is yielding 8½ percent.

3. The company could buy long-term bonds. Long-term governments are yielding almost 6½ percent, and corporate bonds of companies with about the same degree of risk as Texas Land are yielding 8½ percent.

4. The company could buy high-quality preferred stock with yields of about 9 percent.

5. The company could buy common stocks of other companies.

6. The company could buy its own stock in the open market.

7. The company could increase dividends.

Questions

Discuss the pros and cons of the alternatives and make a specific recommendation, including the dollar amounts involved, for the disposal of the excess liquidity.

South-East Marine, Inc.

(Credit Policy and Accounts Receivable Management)

South-East Marine is the largest wholesale distributor of marine parts and equipment in the southeastern United States, serving the region from outlets in Miami, Tampa, Jacksonville, Charleston, Norfolk, Mobile, New Orleans, and Houston. A new management team recently took over the firm, and the new board is now in the process of reviewing the firm's working capital policy. Earlier discussions had established desired levels of overall current assets and current liabilities, or the general working capital policy, and management must now consider specific current asset and liability levels.

On June 15, 1972, a board meeting was called to discuss the firm's credit policy, and the effect of credit policy on accounts receivable. Ralph Burroughs, President and Chairman of the Board, led off the meeting by noting that the current credit policy had been established by the previous management group, and that this policy needed to be reviewed. Richard Chandler, President of the Chandler National Bank of Miami, and a new South-East Marine director, followed Burroughs, stating that he was alarmed over the rising level of bad debt losses, the growing level of receivables, and the increasing cost of collecting overdue accounts. Chandler felt that the past credit policy had been too lenient, and he wanted to see the board establish more rigid guidelines.

Chip Bradley, Vice President, Marketing, and one of the few holdovers from the old management team, interrupted, stating that if growth in sales and profits was to be realized, an easier credit policy should be established. Accordingly, he recommended easing credit terms.

Dick Chandler retorted that with an average margin of 15 percent on sales, the firm has to make six new sales to make up for one credit loss, and that easing terms was more likely to produce the one loss than the six good customers.

When asked his opinion, Al Willard, Vice President-Finance, stated that the financial staff had examined several alternative credit procedures, including the possibility of factoring accounts receivable and/or eliminating the discount for early payment, but it had reached no firm conclusions. Willard also reported that the firm's current credit policy, 2/10 net 30, was similar to that of most other firms in the industry, but that South-East Marine's strong market position would enable it to deviate from industry practices without excessive losses of sales.

At this point, it was obvious that the board needed additional facts before it could reach any decision, so Willard was asked to prepare an analysis of alternative credit policies for presentation at the next board meeting. Willard's analysis is summarized in Figure 31.1 and Tables 31.1 through 31.6. On the basis of his analysis, Willard felt that a generally tighter credit policy should be adopted, and he suggested credit terms of 1/10 net 20, together with a more extensive screening of new accounts.

Although Chip Bradley's staff had provided the sales estimates for the various credit policies, he took issue with Willard's analysis and conclusions. First, he thought that the credit loss percentage was overstated for the easier credit policy and understated for the tighter credit policy. Second, he objected to the 3 percent discount under the "easy credit" policy. Bradley felt that sales were affected primarily by the total time to pay

Figure 31.1

DISTRIBUTION OF CREDIT PAYMENTS OVER TIME
UNDER THE PRESENT POLICY OF 2/10, NET 30

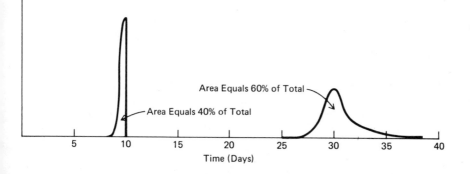

Table 31.1

PROJECTED SALES AND ACCOUNTS RECEIVABLE
UNDER ALTERNATIVE CREDIT POLICIES
($ in Millions)

	Present Policy (2/10, net 30)		Easier Policy (3/15, net 45)		Tighter Policy (1/10, net 20)	
Year ending Dec. 31	*Credit Sales*	*Average Accounts Receivable[a]*	*Credit Sales*	*Average Accounts Receivable[a]*	*Credit Sales*	*Average Accounts Receivable[a]*
1972	20.0	1.670	20.0	2.502	20.0	1.112
1973	22.5	1.875	23.0	2.875	22.2	1.233
1974	25.3	2.108	26.5	3.313	24.6	1.367
		30 days out-standing on Acc. Rec.		45 days out-standing on Acc. Rec.		20 days out-standing on Acc. Rec.

[a] Average accounts receivable are calculated as follows:

$$\text{Avg. A/R} = \left(\frac{\text{Credit Sales}}{360 \text{ Days}}\right)(\text{Average Days Outstanding}).$$

EXAMPLE: 1973, easier policy:

$$\text{Avg. A/R} = \frac{\$23 \text{ Million}}{360}(45) = \$2,875,000.$$

Table 31.2

COST DATA ASSOCIATED WITH
ALTERNATIVE CREDIT POLICIES

	Current Policy 1972	Easier Credit 1973/1974	Tighter Credit 1973/1974
Credit losses as a percentage of sales	2%	3%	1%
Cost of capital[a]	12%	12%	12%
Cash discount	2%	3%	1%
Collection expenses per $1,000 of credit sales	$1.00	$1.50	$0.50
Credit checking costs per $1,000 of credit sales	$0.10	$0.05	$0.20
Profit margin before costs associated with credit	15%	15%	15%
Percentage of customers who take discount	40%	40%	40%

[a] The cost of capital is 12 percent per year.

    Table 31.3

WORKSHEET: PRESENT POLICY

1973 *Profit from Sales*

Sales×Margin: 22.5×.15=		$3,375,000
Expenses of Credit		
a. Credit losses: 22.5×.02=	$450,000	
b. Time value of money tied up in Acc. Rec.: 1.875×.12=	225,000	
c. Discount for early payment: 22.5×.4×.02=	180,000	
d. Collection expenses: 22.5×.001=	22,500	
e. Credit checking costs: 22.5×.0001=	2,250	$ 879,750
Gross profit after credit expenses		$2,495,250

1974 *Profit from Sales*

Sales×Margin: 25.3×.15=		$3,795,000
Expenses of Credit		
a. Credit losses: 25.3×.02=	$506,000	
b. Time value of money tied up in Acc. Rec.: 2.108×.12=	252,960	
c. Discount for early payment: 25.3×.4×.02=	202,400	
d. Collection expenses: 22.5×.001=	25,300	
e. Credit checking costs: 25.3×.0001=	2,530	$ 989,190
Gross profit after credit expenses		$2,805,810

(the "net 30," "net 45," and so on) and the credit standards, and to a much smaller extent by the discount offered for cash payment. According to Bradley, the discount simply amounted to a price reduction, and he did not feel that sales would respond much to such a small price cut.

Willard retorted that the information in the tables was based upon probability distributions of sales for each credit policy as supplied by the sales department and approved by Bradley. After additional discussion, it was decided that (1) the relationships between sales and credit policy were uncertain, but (2) the relationships assumed in the exhibits were reasonable for illustrative purposes.

To illustrate the effects of stretching out the length of the credit period in the event the discount is not taken, Willard pointed out that under the present policy of 2/10 net 30 the effective interest rate was about 36 percent. If the company extended the due date to 40 days, then the effective interest rate would drop to 24 percent. The same drop would occur if the 30-day period was retained but customers were actually allowed to delay payment for 40 days. Thus, a lack of enforcement of whatever policy was accepted would lower the effective interest to the

Table 31.4

WORKSHEET: EASIER CREDIT POLICY

1973 *Profit from Sales*

Sales×Margin: 23.0×.15=		$3,450,000
Expenses of Credit		
a. Credit losses: 23×.03=	$690,000	
b. Time value of money tied up in Acc. Rec.: 2.875×.12=	345,000	
c. Discount for early payment: 23×.4×.03=	276,000	
d. Collection expenses: 23×.0015=	34,500	
e. Credit checking costs: 23×.00005=	1,150	
Gross profit after credit expenses		$2,103,350
Difference from Present Policy		($ 391,900)

1974 *Profit from Sales*

Sales×Margin: 26.5×.15=		$3,975,000
Expenses of Credit		
a. Credit losses: 26.5×.03=	$795,000	
b. Time value of money tied up in Acc. Rec.: 3.313×.12=	397,560	
c. Discount for early payment: 26.5×.4×.03=	318,000	
d. Collection expenses: 26.5×.0015=	39,750	
e. Credit checking costs: 26.5×.00005=	1,325	1,551,635
Gross Profit after credit expenses		$2,423,365
Difference from Present Policy		($ 382,445)

purchasing company, thus tending to increase the average accounts receivable.

Willard also noted that sometimes customers would attempt to take the discount after the discount period had expired, but that one of the first things he had done upon assuming his new position was to stop this practice. The old enforcement policy had been so lax that about 40 percent of the firms taking the discount had actually paid anywhere from 1 to 10 days past the discount period.

Additionally, Willard felt that the discount policy had an important effect on sales—more important than Bradley suggested. Finally, Willard questioned whether it was reasonable to assume that the percentage of credit customers taking the discount would remain the same for each alternative. He did note that the implicit interest rate, which is an essential element in the decision to take the discount, would be about 36 percent for all three of the policies under consideration. Thus, the assumption of a constant percentage of discount customers might not be unreasonable.

Table 31.5

WORKSHEET: TIGHTER CREDIT POLICY

1973 *Profit from Sales*

Sales×Margin: $22.2 \times .15 =$		$3,330,000
Expenses of Credit		
a. Credit Losses: $22.2 \times .01 =$	$222,000	
b. Time value of money tied up in Acc. Rec.: $1.233 \times .12 =$	147,960	
c. Discount for early payment: $22.2 \times .4 \times .01 =$	88,800	
d. Collection expenses: $22.2 \times .0005 =$	11,100	
e. Credit checking costs: $22.2 \times .0002 =$	4,440	$ 474,300
Gross profit after credit expenses		$2,855,700
Difference from Present Policy		$ 360,450

1974 *Profit from Sales*

Sales×Margin: $24.6 \times .15 =$		$3,690,000
Expenses of Credit		
a. Credit losses: $24.6 \times .01 =$	$246,000	
b. Time value of money tied up in Acc. Rec.: $1.367 \times .12 =$	164,040	
c. Discount for early payment: $24.6 \times .4 \times .01 =$	98,400	
d. Collection expenses: $24.6 \times .0005 =$	12,300	
e. Credit checking costs: $24.6 \times .0002 =$	4,920	$ 525,660
Gross profit after credit expenses		$3,164,340
Difference from Present Policy		$ 358,530

Table 31.6

SUMMARY OF DIFFERENCES FROM PRESENT
CREDIT POLICY

Gain or Loss in Gross Profit After Credit-Associated Costs

	Easier Credit Policy (3/15, Net 45)	Tighter Credit Policy (1/10, Net 20)
1973	($391,900)	$360,450
1974	($382,445)	$358,530

Bradley, because he felt that it was not necessary to give a price reduc-tion in the form of an increased discount to encourage a higher level of sales, suggested an alternative easy credit policy calling for 2.5/15, net 45, with an implicit interest rate of 30 percent annually. He felt that this policy would generate about the same sales level as forecast under Willard's illustrative easy credit policy in Table 31.1.

Bradley reiterated that the key to credit sales was not the implicit interest rate of the credit terms, but the time of final payment and the administration of credit standards. Under an easier credit policy, the standards would be lower, thus reducing the cost of credit checking as was illustrated in the exhibits prepared by Al Willard. However, giving consideration to the increased collection efforts as evidenced by an increase in collection expense of 50 percent, he thought that the credit losses would not increase to 3 percent of credit sales. A more realistic figure, according to Bradley, would be about 2½ percent of sales. Additionally, if the discount was changed to 2.5/15 net 45, he felt that only 30 percent of all credit sales would take the discount.

Dick Chandler, who had indicated previously that he thought credit should be tightened, suggested that the Board, on the basis of Willard's analysis, adopt the tighter credit policy. Chandler did, however, note that it would probably be impossible to move from a 2 percent loss rate to a 1 percent rate within one year. Actually, a gradual shift in the loss ratio after the implementation of a tighter policy was more likely.

Ralph Burroughs, while generally pleased with Willard's study, was not ready to take action. He felt that additional data was necessary, so he asked Willard to make the following changes in his tables and resubmit the material at the next Board meeting:

1. Assume that the *sales* shown in Table 31.1 are valid even though other variables change.
2. Drop the discount on an easier credit policy from 3/15, net 45 to 2.5/15, net 45.
3. Assume that the credit losses under the easier policy will be 2.5 percent of credit sales in 1974, and that the losses under both policies will gradually change during the year that the change in credit policy is made. Thus, the data for the 1973 credit loss percentage would be 2.25 percent for the easier credit and 1.5 percent for tighter credit. The 2.5 percent for easier credit and 1.0 percent for tighter credit would be fully realized in 1974.
4. Assume that under the tighter policy (1/10, net 20), 45 percent of credit sales take the discount, but the average collection period remains at 20 days.
5. Under the easier credit policy (2.5/15, net 45), assume that 30 percent of credit customers take the discount, but the average collection period remains at 45 days.
6. Assume that the credit losses under the easier policy will be 2.5 percent of credit sales in 1974.

Questions

1. Reconstruct Table 31.2 to incorporate the changes that Mr. Burroughs has suggested.
2. Develop a new table like 31.4 for easier credit, and a new table like 31.5 for tighter credit, with the new assumption of an average implementation in 1973, change in credit loss percentage, change in discount, and changed percentage of credit sales that take the discount.
3. Make a new summary table like 31.6 to show the differences between the present credit policy, the new easier credit policy, and the new tighter credit policy.
4. Of the variables used in this analysis, which are most likely to be subject to forecasting error?
5. What would be the likely reaction of competitors to each of the proposed changes in credit policy?
6. Draw an approximate distribution of payments over time similar to Figure 31.1 for the easier and tighter policies. Support your reasons for the design of the graphs with a brief discussion.
7. Which policy should be adopted? Why?
8. How should the credit policy which is adopted be implemented? Discuss precise changes in (a) discounts, (b) credit checking standards, and (c) enforcement.

Harding Appliance Company

(Inventory Management)

Harding Appliance Company operates six washer and dryer retail stores in the greater Los Angeles area. The company handles only standard washers and dryers and sells them at a discount below prices in regular department stores. Seasonal sales variations are not pronounced, although there is a peak during the summer months when, because it is a good time to transfer children between schools, people tend to move most frequently. There is also a decline in sales during December and January, when families tend to move least frequently and, in addition, to reduce expenditures on heavy appliances in order to have more funds available for Christmas spending.

Frank Harding, President of Harding Appliance, has always had excellent relations with his bank, the Bank of Los Angeles. However, Gerald Hawk, Vice President and Loan Officer at the bank, recently informed Harding that because of continued tight money in the national economy, the bank would be forced to raise the interest rate on Harding Appliance Company's bank loans from 7½ to 9 percent. Further, Hawk indicated some displeasure at Harding Appliance's recent trends, as shown by the balance sheets in Table 32.1. While Hawk does not plan to take any action to reduce Harding's line of credit at the present time, he has suggested that such action may be necessary in the future if the adverse trends continue and if the supply of money available in the economy remains restricted.

Table 32.1

HARDING APPLIANCE COMPANY
YEAR ENDED DECEMBER 31
(in thousands)

	1967	1968	1969	1970
Cash and marketable securities	$ 210	$ 225	$ 240	$ 256
Accounts receivable	614	625	690	740
Inventories	931	1,070	1,190	1,254
Total current assets	$1,755	$1,920	$2,120	$2,250
Fixed assets	405	420	470	530
Total assets	$2,160	$2,340	$2,590	$2,780
Accounts payable	$ 120	$ 140	$ 175	$ 190
Notes payable	757	849	989	1,081
Total current liabilities	$ 877	$ 989	$1,164	$1,271
Long-term debt	600	600	600	600
Net worth	683	751	826	909
Total liabilities and net worth	$2,160	$2,340	$2,590	$2,780
Sales (thousands)	$4,130	$4,570	$5,001	$5,480
Profits (thousands)	$ 82	$ 74	$ 79	$ 81

When Harding and Hawk were examining the Harding Appliance Company situation, Hawk mentioned that the bank uses a computer program wherein operating data on various customers is fed into the computer, a series of ratios and other forms of analysis are made, and an evaluation of the company, based on trends and comparative data with other firms in the same industry, is given. Hawk indicated to Harding that the computer analysis suggested that Harding's inventories seem to be getting out of line vis-à-vis the rest of the retail appliance industry in the southern California area. (See Table 32.2.)

Table 32.2

INDUSTRY RATIOS, 1970, APPLIANCE RETAILERS[a]

Current ratio	3 to 1
Inventory turnover (sales/inventory)	6 times[b]
Debt ratio (debt/total assets)	60%
Rate of return on net worth	15%
Profit margin (profit/sales)	2%

[a] Industry ratios supplied by Bank of Los Angeles. Industry figures have not changed materially in the past four years.
[b] Sales at retail prices, inventories at cost.

As soon as Harding returned to his office after his discussion at the bank, he called in Ralph Peterson, his comptroller, and asked him to study the financial situation, especially inventories, and to suggest any changes that might be made. Peterson decided to use some of the inventory-evaluation techniques that he had studied in an executive development program given at UCLA a short time before. First, he determined that in 1970 the company had sold 30,000 appliance units at an average cost (*not* sales price) of $150 per unit. The average sales price was $183 per unit. Then Peterson assumed that, in 1971, the average cost and sales price per appliance unit sold would remain constant but that sales would increase to 33,000 units. Further, Peterson calculated costs associated with inventories; these figures are given in Table 32.3. Harding Appliance orders inventory for all six stores together through the central office.

Questions

1. Is the bank's analysis of Harding Appliance Company's inventory position correct; that is, do inventories appear excessive?
2. Calculate the economic order quantity for Harding Appliance under the assumptions of (a) direct ordering from the manufacturer and (b) ordering through the local distributor.
3. How many orders should be placed each year under the assumption (a) that orders are made directly to the manufacturer and (b) that orders are made through the local distributor?
4. What is the reorder point; that is, how low should inventories be permitted to fall before a new order is placed, assuming (a) that it is placed directly with the manufacturer and (b) that it is placed through the local distributor? (Use 360 days a year.)

Table 32.3

HARDING APPLIANCE COMPANY
INVENTORY COSTS

Carrying costs:	Depreciation and obsolescence	12.00%
	Storage and handling	3.50
	Interest (current bank rate)	9.00
	Property taxes	.50
	Insurance	.30
		25.30%
Ordering costs:	Direct from manufacturer,	
	5 days delivery	$200
	Through local distributor,	
	2 days delivery	$150

5. Strikes have been frequent among Harding's suppliers, and the firm is concerned about sales losses due to unavailability of merchandise. Assume that a safety stock of two months' sales must be kept on hand at all times to provide insurance against running out of stock because of strikes, shipping delays, or because of abnormally high sales during the period the firm is awaiting receipt of shipments. How should this affect (a) average inventory held, (b) the cost of ordering and carrying inventory, and (c) the reorder point? Answer questions (b) and (c) in words; do not work out the numbers.

6. What is the average inventory, including the safety stock, in both dollar amounts (at cost) and in units under each of the two alternative methods of ordering?

7. What is the total cost of ordering and carrying inventories under each of the two alternative methods of ordering? Use the following equation: Total cost = carrying cost per unit × average inventory + ordering costs per order × number of orders placed.

8. Which method of ordering inventories should be used?

9. What is the estimated inventory turnover for 1971 assuming (a) the economic order quantity method is used and (b) orders are placed with the local distributor?

10. Is the seasonal sales pattern likely to affect the analysis? If so, how could seasonality be handled?

11. In calculating the cost of carrying inventories, the current rate of interest on bank loans was used. Is this an appropriate procedure?

Case/33

Broadhill Furniture Company

(Financing Current Assets)

In early January 1971, Jason Broadhill, III, Financial Vice President of Broadhill Furniture Company, received a rather disturbing projection from his assistant, Dick Sykes, a new M.B.A. hired last June. The balance sheet that Sykes estimated for 1971, together with the actual balance sheets for 1969 and the one just completed for 1970, are shown in Table 33.1. Certain ratios that Sykes prepared on the basis of the balance sheets and projected income statements (not shown) are given in Table 33.2. Broadhill is very much pleased with the projections of the rate of return on net worth, but he is disturbed by the declining profit margin on sales, the falling rate of return on assets, and, especially, the deteriorating liquidity position and markedly higher projected debt ratio.

Broadhill Furniture Company, a nationally known manufacturer of high-quality furniture items, is located in Lanier, North Carolina. Established in 1893, the company has grown steadily since that time. In 1969, however, the decision was made to embark on a rapid expansion program to capitalize on a new line of furniture developed and patented by the company, which had been very well received by the trade. The expansion program called for increases in assets of approximately 50 percent in each of the years 1970 and 1971.

As Broadhill studied the projections Sykes had given him, his concern increased. Most disconcerting is the liquidity position at the end of 1970,

162

Table 33.1

BROADHILL FURNITURE COMPANY
YEAR ENDED DECEMBER 31
(in millions)

	1969	1970	Estimated 1971
Cash	$ 3.1	$ 4.5	$ 5.0
Accounts receivable	15.1	22.4	44.2
Inventories: Raw materials	2.1	3.2	3.7
Work in process	18.2	26.9	44.6
Finished goods	1.1	1.7	2.5
Total inventories	21.4	31.8	50.8
Total current assets	$ 39.6	$ 58.7	$100.0
Fixed assets	34.7	51.5	60.0
Total assets	$ 74.3	$110.2	$160.0
Accounts payable	$ 6.6	$ 22.4	$ 59.3
Notes payable (Bank: 8%)	10.0	10.0	10.0
Total current liabilities	16.6	32.4	69.3
Long-term debt	11.0	25.0	30.0
Net worth	46.7	52.8	60.7
Total liabilities and net worth	$ 74.3	$110.2	$160.0
Sales	$147	$218	$323

Table 33.2

BROADHILL FURNITURE COMPANY

	1969	1970	Estimated 1971	Industry Average (1970)
Collection period	37 days	37 days	49 days	40 days
Current ratio	2.4 times	1.8 times	1.4 times	2.0 times
Quick ratio	1.1 times	0.8 times	0.7 times	1.0 times
Debt ratio	37.1%	52.1%	62.1%	40.0%
Profit margin on sales	5.1%	4.8%	4.3%	4.0%
Rate of return on assets	10.1%	9.5%	8.7%	9.0%
Rate of return on net worth	16.0%	19.8%	22.9%	15.0%

which is below the level prescribed by the company's board of directors. The level projected for the end of 1971 is entirely out of the question; something will have to be done to increase the current and quick ratios. The debt ratio is worrisome, to say the least, but Broadhill had anticipated this development. In fact, the rising debt ratio was discussed at the last directors' meeting, and the decision was made to let the ratio climb to the level shown for 1971. The directors did, however, agree to consider a cut in the dividend until the debt ratio has been reduced to approximately the level of the industry average, but final action has not been taken on this point.

Broadhill had foreseen neither the declining profit margin on sales nor the falling rate of return on assets. In fact, he had counted on increases in both of these items because of the increased level of efficiency provided by the plant modernization and expansion program. As he studies the figures, however, Broadhill realizes why these declines have occurred. During 1970 the company abandoned its policy of taking cash discounts on all purchases. This loss of discounts—the firm purchased materials on terms of 2/10 net 30—caused an increase in cost and a resulting decline in profit margins and rates of return.

Broadhill's conviction that some important changes must be made, and quickly, is reinforced when his secretary brings him a letter from the insurance company that holds Broadhill Furniture's long-term debt. It states some concern over the declining liquidity position and points out that the agreement under which the loan was made calls for Broadhill to maintain a current ratio of at least 2 to 1. The letter closes by stating that Broadhill is expected to correct the liquidity situation in the very near future. As Broadhill interprets it, if he can devise a plan wherein the liquidity ratios will be corrected within a reasonable period of time, the insurance company will give the firm time to correct the deficiency.

Broadhill's first reaction is that it may be necessary for the company to slow down its expansion program. However, the more he thinks about it, the more difficult this alternative appears. In the first place, the company has already contracted for the fixed assets expansion, so it is impossible to reduce the $60 million figure anticipated for 1971. The company could slow down its rate of growth in sales by turning down orders, and this would enable it to reduce the estimated figures for working capital—cash, accounts receivable, and inventories—for 1971. However, if orders were turned down, the company would be failing to make profitable sales, which would obviously hurt the profit figures, and, in addition, would be creating some ill will that would hurt future operations. This makes the alternative of slowing down sales highly undesirable.

Turning to the liability side of the financial statement, Broadhill recognizes that the anticipated level of accounts payable will present two problems. First, the $59.3 million accounts payable that Skyes has projected for 1971 is based on the assumption that accounts payable will not be paid until 30 days past their due date. Although Sykes has indicated that such delays are common in the industry, Broadhill feels that delayed payments would be harmful to his company. As it now stands, Broadhill Furniture has the reputation of being an excellent customer, and its suppliers make every effort to give Broadhill not only quick delivery but also, during shortage periods, first call on available supplies. Further, because of its reputation as a responsible company, Broadhill has been able to negotiate favorable prices in its supply contracts. If it becomes a slow-paying account, as Sykes' projections would have it, these intangible benefits would be lost. The second problem with the accounts payable projections, of course, is that Broadhill would continue to lose the trade discounts, as it did during 1970.

One way of reducing the accounts payable would be to increase notes payable to banks. Broadhill, in 1970, did attempt to borrow additional funds from the Bank of Lanier, with which the firm has been dealing since it was founded, but this bank was not able to make additional loans to Broadhill because it has capital and surplus of only $100 million and cannot lend more than 10 percent of this amount to any one customer. Because of this limitation, Broadhill has been considering establishing relations with a larger bank in New York or Chicago. Discussions with James Waterford, President of the Bank of Lanier, suggest that additional bank loans at a 10 percent rate from a New York or Chicago bank are entirely feasible. Under the proposed bank loan, Broadhill would be required to give a blanket pledge on all assets that are not already used as security for existing loans. Further, the bank loan could not be granted if either accounts receivable discounting or factoring is employed.

Broadhill also has been informed that he can obtain a loan secured by accounts receivable from a major finance company. The interest rate on such a loan would be 10 percent if accounts receivables are pledged for the loan, and 10 percent plus a 4 percent discount from the face value of each accounts receivable invoice if the credit is obtained by factoring the receivables on a nonrecourse basis. Since his company has its own well-developed credit department, Broadhill questions the wisdom of factoring accounts receivables.

As another alternative that may be feasible, Broadhill is also considering the use of commercial paper. He has noted in recent issues of the *Wall Street Journal* that commercial paper rates at the present time are approximately 7½ percent. In the past few years commercial paper dealers have contacted Broadhill every two or three months to ask whether he was interested in obtaining funds through the commercial paper market, but he has not received any solicitation from these dealers within the last six months.

Finally, Broadhill wonders about the possibility of obtaining credit secured by his inventories. They are projected to rise to almost $51 million by the end of 1971, and, if a lower rate of interest could be obtained by virtue of the fact that the loan would be secured by his inventories, Broadhill would be willing to use them as collateral.

There is no possibility of selling additional long-term debt. The loan agreement with the insurance company calls for Broadhill Furniture to receive an additional $5 million during 1971, but it specifies that the company can obtain no other new long-term financing. Also, because of depressed conditions in the stock market, the board of directors has decreed that there will be no new common stock issues during 1971.

Questions

1. Does the commercial paper market now present a feasible alternative to Broadhill Furniture?
2. Is inventory financing feasible for the company? If so, what form of security arrangements would probably be used?
3. What do you think of Sykes' proposal for allowing accounts payable to build up?
4. Discuss the pros and cons of Broadhill Furniture using accounts receivable financing at the present time. If it elects to use receivables financing, would it be better off to factor receivables or to use an accounts receivable discounting program?
5. Should Broadhill Furniture establish relations and arrange a line of credit with a larger bank?
6. Could a better credit collection program help Broadhill Furniture?
7. What specific actions do you think Jason Broadhill should recommend for the Broadhill Furniture Company during the coming year?

Part / VI

Special Topics in Financial Management

Intertec Incorporated

(Mergers)

Davis Kelly, Assistant to the President of Intertec, Inc., and Barry Blenker, a partner in the consulting firm of Wesley, Wyler & Associates, are, at the request of the Intertec board of directors, preparing a report on the feasibility of Intertec's embarking on a merger and acquisition program. Kelly has an excellent knowledge of Intertec's strengths and weaknesses, while Blenker has had a considerable amount of experience in helping firms locate suitable merger partners and consummate "happy marriages." They are, therefore, a well-balanced team for purposes of formulating Intertec's merger policy.

Intertec was founded in the late 1800s to manufacture a wide variety of precision machine tools, many of them special-purpose machines designed and built to order for individual customers. Since the company is a capital goods producer, its sales have tended to be cyclical; however, during the decade of the 1960s, only one slump, in 1969, had interrupted the company's relatively steady growth (see Tables 34.1 and 34.2). Long recognized as one of the leaders in developing managerial talent, Intertec has a strong, balanced team of management personnel. In fact, the company has more people qualified for responsible positions than it has openings, and to keep them productive is one of the major reasons for considering a merger and acquisition program.

In the report that Kelly and Blenker have outlined and are now putting

Table 34.1

INTERTEC, INCORPORATED
YEAR ENDED 'DECEMBER 31, 1972
(in millions)

Current assets	$ 57.1
Fixed assets	57.2
	$114.3
Current liabilities[a]	$ 14.3
Long-term debt	20.5
Common equity (3 million shares outstanding)	79.5
	$114.3

[a] Includes $10 million in 8 percent bank notes payable which are a "fixed" component of the firm's structure.

Table 34.2

STATISTICAL DATA ON INTERTEC

Year	Sales (millions)	Net Income after Taxes[a] (millions)	Earnings per Share	Dividends per Share	Average Price of Stock
1972	$190	$8.6	$2.87	$1.80	$43
1971	180	8.1	2.70	1.50	39
1970	165	7.6	2.53	1.40	36
1969	130	(2.0)	(.66)	1.40	25
1968	150	6.8	2.27	1.40	34
1967	142	6.5	2.17	1.25	31
1966	134	6.1	2.03	1.25	30
1965	125	5.7	1.90	1.25	28
1964	121	5.5	1.83	1.25	27
1963	113	5.0	1.67	1.00	25
1962	106	4.8	1.60	1.00	24

[a] Assumes a 50 percent marginal tax rate.

into final form, they first considered mergers versus internal growth. Before calling in Wesley, Wyler for advice, Intertec decided to take positive action to increase the firm's rate of growth. Kelly and Blenker reviewed the thinking that went into this decision and concluded that the decision to step up the growth rate was, in fact, a good one. There is, however, a question whether internal growth or growth through mergers would be preferable.

After a careful review of the advantages and disadvantages of mergers vis-à-vis internal growth, Kelly and Blenker concluded that Intertec is expanding its normal product lines as rapidly as possible. Therefore, to achieve a faster growth rate the company must start new divisions in new product areas. Even though it now has the management depth to supply management teams to newly formed divisions, getting such divisions started would be a relatively long, drawn-out process. Then too, since the company would have no experience whatever in the new divisions, there is the strong possibility that costly mistakes would be made. Thus the risk of internal expansion into new product lines is relatively high.

A merger program, on the other hand, would enable Intertec to meet its growth objectives much faster than would a program of internal expansion. And, assuming the prospects of the acquired company are carefully checked before consummating the merger, risk could be reduced. In addition, Kelly and Blenker feel that there are potential merger candidates whose current earnings are being held down by a relatively poor management. If Intertec were to take over such a company and bolster the company's management with some of its own personnel, earnings would quite likely increase. In other words, Kelly and Blenker feel that in some cases they would be able to purchase more productive capacity per dollar expended via the merger route than via internal expansion. Of course, they recognize that it is also possible to pay too much when acquiring a firm, but they are confident that Intertec will be able to separate good from bad mergers.

Aside from the synergistic aspects of proposed mergers—and Kelly and Blenker recognize that synergistic effects are of the utmost importance—the terms of a merger are clearly the most important financial consideration. Although merger with a firm in a high-growth industry would boost Intertec's total growth rate, such a firm is likely to be selling at a higher price-earnings ratio than Intertec, which might well cause an initial dilution in earnings per share. On the other hand, Intertec might purchase a company that has relatively poor earnings prospects but is selling at a low price-earnings multiple, and this could provide Intertec with an immediate earnings increase.

Kelly and Blenker recognize that major factors come into play when setting the price to be paid for the stock.[1] Certainly relative earnings, dividends, growth rates, book value per share, and market price are all important considerations.

Rather than generalizing about these factors in their report, Kelly and Blenker decide to discuss the terms that might be applied to four potential merger candidates that have come to their attention. Some statistics on the four firms in question are presented in Table 34.3. A brief description of each of the companies follows.

---

[1] In an exchange of stock, the "price" per share paid for the candidate is the fair market value of the Intertec stock divided by the number of shares acquired from the candidate.

Table 34.3

STATISTICS ON POTENTIAL MERGER CANDIDATES
DECEMBER 31, 1972

| | | | Per Share | | | | |
	Earnings	Dividends	Growth Rate (EPS and DPS)	Book Value	Market Price	Number of Shares Outstanding	Debt Ratio
Foster Pump Co.	$1.65	$1.00	7%	$33	$52	1,000,000	35%
Iowa Implements	4.20	3.50	1%	55	41	2,000,000	10%
Space Technology	1.20	—	15%	14	54	100,000	50%
Akron Machine Co.	3.00	1.50	3%	29	39	1,000,000	20%

Foster Pump Company

Foster Pump Company manufactures a line of pumps used in irrigation, flood control, and similar applications. E. F. Foster, Chairman of the Board, would probably resist a merger offer, but Foster has direct control of only 15 percent of the stock, with the other stock being widely distributed. To take over the Foster Pump Company, Intertec would probably have to overcome the resistance of management and would probably have to resort to a tender offer.

Iowa Implements Company

Iowa Implements Company is a manufacturer of tractors, harrows, plows, and other farm implements. The company is generally recognized as a laggard in its industry. Its chief weaknesses, aside from top management, are thought to lie in product design, production processes (production costs are higher than they should be), and lack of an adequate sales financing plan. The company has a strong dealer distribution system with a good maintenance and repair service reputation. Kelly is aware that at least two other firms considered acquiring Iowa Implements but decided against the purchase because Iowa Implements' deep-seated problems would put a drain on the time and energy of their own managements. Iowa Implements' management would not resist a merger.

Space Technology

Space Technology Corporation is a new firm engaged primarily in supplying high-quality metallurgical products to major aerospace companies. Although the aerospace industry as a whole is having a difficult time, Space Technology is not. The company already has a research and development contract with NASA and, assuming preliminary findings are borne out, a long-term contract for heat shields to be used in the Venus program will be forthcoming. In addition to the company's own growth and earnings potential, Kelly and Blenker believe that some of the metallurgical processes being developed by Space Technology would also benefit Intertec's primary product line. Forty percent of Space Technology's common stock is owned by its board chairman, with its president owning an additional 20 percent of the stock. While these two men have indicated that they are willing to discuss a merger, they have made it clear that they will agree to one only if the price is relatively high.

Akron Machine Company

The Akron Machine Company manufactures equipment used in tire-retreading operations. Although the company's products are good and it is relatively well run, the retread business is one that prospers when consumer incomes are low, so the company's growth rate in recent years has been slower than that of the general economy. Rumors have recently been circulating that Southwest Industries, a major conglomerate, is planning to make a tender offer for Akron's stock and that Akron's management is opposed to a merger with Southwest. Kelly and Blenker think that Akron's management may well welcome a merger offer from Intertec to avoid being taken over by Southwest.

Questions

1. For each prospective merger candidate determine an appropriate price per share which Intertec should pay. Approach the problem from the standpoint of a cost of capital/capital budgeting investment decision to determine numerical values per share. Assume that Space Technology's recent growth will last for 8 years with no payout, after which growth will fall to 6 percent with a 50 percent payout. Also, assume that Intertec can sell new debt at a rate of 8 percent. Alternatively, the firm could finance its acquisition(s) with an exchange of stock. Flotation costs under either method would be close to zero. (HINT: First calculate Intertec's cost of capital. Then use this figure, together with the target companies' dividends and projected growth figures to determine price per share figures for the merger candidates.)

2. Discuss the feasibility of actually acquiring these firms at the prices you computed. What other factors might change your initial valuation figures? Discuss specifically such questions as the size of the potential merger, changes in the firm's overall risk characteristics, possible effects on its cost of capital, synergistic effects from the merger, and changes in growth potential.

3. Assume that management decides to merge with either Foster Pump or Iowa Implements. Since Iowa Implements' management favors a merger, assume that they will support Intertec's bid for an exchange of stock at market price. For Foster Pump, assume that Intertec makes a tender offer of stock at a 15 percent premium over market price to insure the success of the offer. For the two possible mergers, compute (a) Intertec's share exchange ratio, (b) new growth rate in earnings, and (c) new earnings per share for the first year after the merger (assume no synergistic effects).

4. For each merger candidate, indicate what strategy should be used in the takeover and how the merger should be financed, i.e., debt or equity.

5. All things considered, including possible synergistic effects, which

mergers should Blenker and Kelly recommend to Intertec's management?

6. The discount rate you used in evaluating the candidates was Intertec's weighted cost of capital. How valid is this rate for a large merger candidate? Ideally, how would Intertec attempt to determine an appropriate discount rate?

B. F. Goodrich[1]

(Mergers)

When Northwest Industries announced a $1-billion tender offer for B. F. Goodrich last January, many experts considered the case as good as closed. Even though Goodrich is a giant corporation with 1968 sales of $1.1 billion, with forty plants in the U.S. and interests in twenty-six foreign countries, it looked like easy picking. The Northwest offer, a complicated package of stock, warrants, and debentures, was worth 30 percent more than the market value of Goodrich common stock. But, as Northwest quickly discovered, a take-over is no longer a matter of tempting stockholders and arbitrageurs with a quick profit.

Goodrich was to be helped immeasurably, of course, by a rising antimerger attitude in Washington. While the Northwest tender offer was in effect, the Justice Department filed an antitrust suit seeking to block the merger. Congress meanwhile announced an impending investigation of conglomerates. And Congressman Wilbur Mills, powerful chairman of the House Ways and Means Committee, introduced legislation to limit the use of interest-bearing debentures in tenders.

---

[1] This case appeared as an article in *Fortune* (Tom O'Hanlon, "Goodrich's Four-Ply Defense," *Fortune,* July 1969, pp. 110–114).

While the outcome of the struggle was in the balance as this article went to press, Goodrich's efforts to fend off Northwest's take-over rank as a case study in defensive tactics. Shortly after the Northwest offer became public, Jefferson Ward Keener, the dour chairman and chief executive officer of Goodrich, gathered a group of legal, financial, and public-relations experts to stop Northwest. A seven-page confidential memorandum dated January 31, 1969, circulated among five top executives of Goodrich, tells the conclusions the experts reached. "The general consensus of our advisers has remained unchanged," reads the memorandum, "namely that we do not have much chance of warding off Northwest Industries (NW) unless there is some legal quirk that is peculiar to this situation, or unless we merge with a friendly party or parties, which would result in our stockholders getting a better deal than the package NW has offered." The better deal never materialized, but the delaying strategy outlined in the memorandum kept Northwest at bay for months and allowed Washington to come galloping to the rescue of the besieged Akron management.

Among the tactics proposed in the memorandum was the acquisition of a trucking company operating in the area served by the Chicago & North Western Railway, one of Northwest's principal subsidiaries. The idea was to place Goodrich under the jurisdiction of the ICC, which in turn might have barred the merger because it would have put Northwest in control of two competing modes of transportation. Several court actions were also recommended, including a suit alleging violations by Northwest of the Securities Exchange Act, and a suit charging infringement of the antitrust act. Goodrich was advised to acquire smaller companies with the idea of getting more than 20 percent of the company's stock in friendly hands, thereby preventing Northwest from filing a consolidated income-tax report. The memorandum noted that the company had already taken steps to alter its arrangement with a group of banks so that a $200-million credit line would be in default in the event that Northwest managed to get control. As the document shows, Goodrich was also considering efforts to have Northwest delisted by the New York Stock Exchange, and hoped to instigate a congressional investigation of "funny-money" take-overs.

Much of the subsequent action followed the Goodrich script. Goodrich acquired a trucking company and asked the ICC to intervene in the take-over fight—a request that was turned down. Northwest had said it would sell the trucking company if it gained control of Goodrich. Stock was placed in friendly hands when Goodrich acquired Gulf Oil's half interest in a jointly owned synthetic rubber plant in exchange for 700,000 of its shares. Stockholders meanwhile approved the classification of directors into three groups, plus a system of cumulative voting designed to keep Northwest from taking immediate control if its tender offer was successful. The stockholders balked, however, at management's proposal that the vote required to permit the acquisition of Goodrich by a company that management opposed be raised from a two-thirds majority of shares outstanding to 80 percent.

"THIS IS GROSS IMPROPRIETY"

In its counterattack, Goodrich was helped by a few serious problems at Northwest. The company began losing money in the first quarter of 1969 because of a strike at its Lone Star Steel Co. and severe weather that affected freight operations on the Chicago & North Western. Northwest stock, which had been selling at $138 a share, had fallen to $105 by the end of February. Moreover, the restriction in the Mills bill prompted Ben W. Heineman, Northwest's president and chief executive, to revise the terms of his offer by decreasing the amount of debt and by increasing the amount of common stock and warrants in the package.

In May came the news that Goodrich executives had been long awaiting —the Justice Department brought that antitrust suit seeking to enjoin Northwest from acquiring Goodrich. That action was hardly news to Keener and his associates. In February, Goodrich had added to its battery of legal talent the Chicago firm of Chadwell, Keck, Kayser & Ruggles in connection with a suit filed by Northwest that was unrelated to the antitrust case. Richard W. McLaren had resigned from the firm in January to become head of the Justice Department's Antitrust Division. A copy of a letter from McLaren to Northwest's lawyers, dealing with antitrust aspects of the attempted take-over, had been sent to his former colleague, John Chadwell. The letter enabled both Goodrich and Northwest to estimate the date of a possible antitrust suit.

For the Northwest executives, the antitrust suit was the last straw. Heineman felt that his tender offer would have prevailed despite the ingenuity of the Goodrich defense. "This is gross impropriety," said Heineman. "I think Mr. Chadwell should not have accepted the case, or that Mr. McLaren should have disqualified himself." McLaren subsequently replied that the suit was unanimously recommended by members of his staff, and that he had left the Chadwell firm before it was retained by Goodrich. Moreover, he asserted that it is normal to keep all parties advised in such cases.

A TEMPTING TARGET

Over the years Goodrich has been a lackluster performer. Its profits last year were nearly $2 million less than the $46 million earned back in 1955, although sales had increased by 51 percent over the same period. Measured against its competitors in Akron, Goodrich is a poor last. Since 1958, earnings per share have increased at an average annual growth rate of only 2.14 percent, far below the 7.96 percent of Goodyear and the 8.7 percent of Firestone. The Goodrich margin on sales averaged 4.1 percent compared to 4.8 percent for Goodyear and 5.3 percent for Firestone. And the company's 8.1 percent return on invested capital last year lagged far behind Firestone's 12.6 percent and Goodyear's 12.8 percent. The Goodrich management was well aware of its faltering performance, and twice in the past five years made some bold efforts to improve earnings. But none of these efforts was really successful. Even before Northwest Industries made its move, Goodrich was an ideal target for an aggressive conglomerate.

A conservative economist who became chief executive officer in 1958, Chairman Keener for years kept a lid on capital spending at a time when the competition was borrowing heavily to expand. Until recent years, Keener, like his predecessor John Lyon Collyer, disliked the idea of incurring long-term debt, even though cash flow was insufficient to finance expansion at a pace comparable to that of the other rubber companies. On the other hand, Keener had no objection to paying out as much as 76 percent of Goodrich's earnings to stockholders. One result of niggardly capital spending can be seen in a key statistic. Goodrich labor costs in relation to sales are 35.1 percent, compared to 30.2 percent for Goodyear. For a billion-dollar company, each tenth of a percentage point in cost reductions represents $1 million a year increase in pre-tax profits.

Though Goodrich is best known as a tire manufacturer, 60 percent of its sales and earnings come from other fields. In the Fifties the chemical industry was a logical field of expansion since Goodrich, from the days before World War II when it pioneered in the development of synthetic rubber, had a strong research staff. The most important, and initially the most profitable, venture in chemicals was the manufacture of polyvinyl chloride (PVC), a basic building block in plastics. One of the first companies to market this material, Goodrich priced PVC so that profit margins were extremely high, balm indeed in view of the unexciting profits in the tire business. As new applications were found for the plastic, the market grew rapidly and Goodrich spent heavily to expand production. But more chemical companies, attracted by the high profits and strong growth, began making PVC and prices tumbled sharply. In 1954 general-purpose PVC sold for 38 cents a pound; last year the average price was 10 cents. Goodrich is still the world's largest producer of PVC and has the lowest-cost manufacturing process, but there is a widespread belief that its pricing policies of the Fifties (set by Keener's predecessor) may have invited competitors into the field too soon.

A more recent effort in chemicals has been unsuccessful, at least so far. In the mid-Sixties, scientists at the Goodrich research center near Akron developed a poromeric material with many of the characteristics of Du

Pont's Corfam. After some development work, a pilot plant was begun, and the product, named Aztran, seemed commercially salable. In 1967 a multimillion-dollar plant was built in Marietta, Ohio, and salesmen began making the rounds of shoe manufacturers. Sales were disappointing, however, since Goodrich offered Aztran for men's shoes only, while Du Pont had developed several kinds of Corfam that conformed in price and appearance to the many kinds of leather available. Although an effort is now being made to develop a range similar to Corfam, Goodrich executives are considering the possibility of writing off the Aztran adventure.

Goodrich is engaged in a multiplicity of other endeavors. It makes a variety of industrial chemicals, is a major producer of synthetic rubber, and has fourteen industrial-product plants that produce everything from rubber bands to mattresses. About 5 percent of sales come from a footwear division, 5 percent from aerospace, and 2 percent from textiles. Finally, about 13 percent of Goodrich sales come from its international operations.

RUSHING THE RADIAL AGE

The rapid growth of foreign markets is the most exciting aspect of the tire business these days, but Goodrich is in poor position to cash in on the boom. The company was reluctant to invest heavily abroad after World War II, and even in the Fifties its European investment consisted of minority interests in manufacturers, such as Kleber-Colombes in France and Veith in West Germany. Today American companies control a major portion of the foreign tire business, mainly because Firestone and Goodyear saw unparalleled opportunity. These two companies together own or have an interest in sixty-two foreign plants while Goodrich controls seven foreign factories and has minority interests in five other tire plants. Goodrich's first wholly owned European tire plant, located in West Germany, began full production only a few months ago.

In its tire business at home, Goodrich has blown hot and cold. When Goodyear cut tire prices by 10 to 15 percent in 1959, Goodrich was handicapped with high-cost, inefficient plants, the legacy of the company's pinch-penny policies. Not until 1962 did it build a modern plant in Fort Wayne, Indiana, and by then the competition had taken away a good slice of the business. (The decline in Goodrich's market share is well known in the industry, though rubber companies refuse to give any figures.) Moreover, Goodrich depended heavily on sales of original-equipment tires to Detroit auto manufacturers and allowed the competition to cream the larger and more lucrative replacement market. Firestone and Goodyear both spent heavily to build their own outlets, while Goodrich made a stab at improving its marketing strength by making two small acquisitions in 1961—Rayco Stores with 124 outlets, and Vanderbilt Tire, which had franchise arrangements with department stores in major cities. Vanderbilt was sold in 1965, and with Rayco, Goodrich has about half as many retail outlets as either Firestone or Goodyear. Yet it must mount a costly national advertising program to keep up with these two giants.

At times Goodrich has run its tire busines as if it wanted sales at any price. Consider the Goodrich tactics in bidding to supply tires for Detroit's municipally owned buses. In such cases tire companies try to sell contractual mileage accounts, under which fleet owners lease tires with charges based on tire usage. For thirty-five years Uniroyal had won the contract, but in 1963, Goodrich won with a bid worth $1,450,000 over five years, about $195,000 below Uniroyal. That low bid was enhanced by the elimination of a wage escalation clause, which the other companies considered necessary because of the certainty of higher labor costs. Last year Goodrich won the contract again by bidding at the same price, and it must absorb all wage increase granted until 1973. Goodrich insists that it is breaking even on the contract. But a competitor who dropped out of the bidding insists that it is impossible to make a profit at Goodrich's price.

Two years ago Goodrich made an expensive gamble in an effort to improve its position in the tire industry. Believing that Detroit would adopt a European-style radial tire as standard equipment on many new cars in 1971, Goodrich tooled up for what appeared to be a large and profitable market. The radial tire requires special manufacturing equipment and techniques, and Goodrich plunged ahead. The other tire makers, however, chose to put their bets on the belted bias tire, a reinforced version of the conventional two-ply tire.

While acknowledging the radial tire's safer riding characteristics and longer mileage, Detroit's experts had two objections to the Goodrich tire. First, it costs considerably more than conventional equipment. More important, engineers felt that radials (highly popular in Europe) were incompatible with the suspension systems of the best-selling American cars, producing a harsh ride. But even if the riding characteristics of the tire were acceptable, it is doubtful that the automobile companies would feel comfortable with a single source of supply. The fact that Goodyear, Firestone, and others failed to build sizable capacity for making the radial tire probably doomed in advance the Goodrich idea of selling radials as original equipment. While still insisting on the superiority of the radial tire, Goodrich now concedes that the belted bias tire will be standard equipment on most U.S.-made cars in the years just ahead.

SPRINGING THE TRAP

When Heineman took a look at Goodrich last fall, he saw a matchless opportunity for a major acquisition. A staff group headed by

Howard A. Newman, chairman of the board of Northwest, had made a lengthy analysis of Goodrich. It had a low debt-equity ratio, and despite its wobbly earnings record, an important position in both the chemical and the tire industries. Heineman believed that the company, with its untapped earnings potential, was undervalued by the investment community. Most important of all, Heineman concluded that the company's poor performance was attributable to the lack of aggressive management.

Heineman hesitated for about two months to move on Goodrich, partly because he also had his eye on another company. Without revealing the name, he had received the approval of Northwest's board for open-market purchases in Interchemical (which has since changed its name to Inmont), a New York-based chemical company with sales of $317 million and earnings of $14,200,000. After accumulating just under 10 percent of Interchemical stock, Heineman called on President James T. Hill to inform him of the fact, and to tell him that Northwest had not decided what course of action to pursue. It was clear from the conversation, however, that Hill would have rebuffed any take-over bid.

On December 23 the executive committee of the Northwest board approved the purchase of 350,000 shares, or about 2.5 percent of the shares then outstanding. One of the board members, Laurence A. Tisch, chairman and chief executive officer of Loew's Theaters Inc., was playing tennis that day at his Paradise Island hotel in the Bahamas. His game was interrupted by a telephone call from Newman, who asked his approval of the purchase and described the reasons for the investment. "There's no need to go through all that, Mickey," said Tisch. "I know all about the company. We have a large position." As it happened, Loew's had been buying Goodrich stock for a number of months and had accumulated 358,450 shares. From that point on, however, Loew's stopped buying. Goodrich has since charged that Heineman and Tisch were acting in collusion in their stock purchases. Both are vehement in their denials. "It simply looked to me as if Goodrich had little downside risk," says Tisch. "It just looked like a good investment."

The heavy buying in Goodrich stock attracted the attention of John L. Weinberg, a Goodrich director and a partner in Goldman, Sachs. The previous June, Weinberg had arranged a meeting between Keener and Delbert W. Coleman, who then was president of Seeberg Corp., a jukebox manufacturer. Coleman wanted to present a merger idea to Goodrich. The proposal was rejected, but Weinberg recalls that he warned Keener, "Ward, this is the kind of world you're living in today." On January 9, Tisch disclosed that Loew's had a position in Goodrich, and although he disclaimed any intention of making a tender offer, the atmosphere in Akron grew tense. "I didn't try to hide my investment in Goodrich," says Tisch. "I was buying in the fall through Goldman, Sachs."

However, neither Keener nor Weinberg could be sure that Loew's alone was responsible for all the buying of Goodrich stock.

A DEAL AT A DINNER PARTY

At that point, Keener decided that Goodrich should think of opening negotiations with potential merger partners of its own choice. That triggered an episode of comic misadventure that is a source of embarrassment to some of the participants, and there are conflicting versions of the incident. Apparently misunderstanding the instructions of a Goodrich executive, the accounting firm of Ernst & Ernst, which had previously been commissioned to seek acquisitions for Goodrich, asked Lehman Brothers to suggest companies that might be suitably combined with its Akron client.

At a dinner party in New York on Friday, January 10, three weeks after Northwest had begun buying Goodrich stock, Robert McCabe, a partner in Lehman Brothers, was a dinner guest of Alan Patricof, assistant to the chairman of the board of Northwest Industries. Patricof was dumfounded when the man from Lehman Brothers asked if Northwest might be interested in making a deal with Goodrich. At that point Northwest owned 156,000 shares of Goodrich. With understandable eagerness, Patricof led his guest to a telephone and McCabe had a lengthy conversation with Stephen Dubrul, another Lehman Brothers partner. As a result, Lehman Brothers recommended that Ernst & Ernst propose Northwest to the Goodrich management.

The real intentions of Goodrich at that point are known only to Keener and his associates. Heineman, however, took the Lehman Brothers proposal at face value, a signal that the Akron management was ready to talk. He therefore requested that Northwest be given the first opportunity to negotiate with Goodrich. But Lehman Brothers could not give preferential treatment to Northwest, saying only that the company's name would be submitted along with about a dozen others. And however much Heineman may have wanted a confidential chat with Keener, the ethical conventions of the financial world prevented Northwest from bypassing the two middlemen and making its offer directly to Goodrich.

Unknown to Heineman, his interest was conveyed almost immediately to Goodrich anyway. During a flight from New York to Akron on Monday, January 13, John Hart, Goodrich's vice controller and a vice president, was informed of the Northwest proposal by an executive from Ernst & Ernst. Hart dismissed the idea, saying vaguely that Goodrich had no intention of going into the railroad business. For some unaccountable reason, Hart failed to report the Northwest proposal to Keener. That breakdown in communication was to become an angry point of dispute in the events that followed.

THE MICE WERE NIBBLING ON WALL STREET

Fearful that some other company might close a deal with Goodrich, the Northwest executives began to think in terms of a tender offer. They decided that an exchange of common stock, warrants, and debentures worth between $75 and $80 for each share of Goodrich common would be attractive enough to gain control. Goodrich stock had been selling in the forties for the last half of 1968, but under the pressure of buying by Northwest had risen to the mid-fifties. However, Heineman had not yet decided whether, or when, he would make an announcement of a tender offer. He still hoped that a friendly deal might be arranged.

Heineman's hand was forced on Firday, January 17. Gustave Levy of Goldman, Sachs telephoned Heineman and said, "Ben, it's all over the Street that you're going to make a tender offer for Goodrich. Is it true?" After a pause, Heineman replied, "I can't comment on that." A few minutes later, an agitated Levy called again with the same question and received this enigmatic reply: "I wouldn't want to put a friend of mine in a position of conflict of interest." Heineman realized that unless he made an announcement of a tender offer, he might be in violation of both SEC and New York Stock Exchange rules on disclosure, and he released the news before the opening of the New York Stock Exchange on Monday, January 20. "I knew on Friday that we had to move," Heineman recalled later. "The mice were nibbling all over Wall Street and both Northwest and Goodrich stocks were rising."

Keener was infuriated when he read the details of the Northwest offer that morning. "They have started off on the wrong foot," he said, "regardless of whether or not their proposal has any merit." Heineman says he tried to soften the blow by telephoning Keener that morning prior to publication of the offer, but was unable to reach him. Moreover, Heineman waved the olive branch in his press release by stating that Northwest had no intention of altering the Goodrich management. In a further gesture of conciliation, Larry Tisch told Gus Levy that Northwest would propose a new exchange offer if Goodrich was willing to make a friendly deal, and that there was a chance that Goodrich could be the surviving company. Keener rebuffed these overtures. A Goodrich director says, "Heineman knew where the hell we were. If he really wanted to be friendly—well, you don't sneak around behind someone and hit him over the head with a baseball bat, and then run around in front and say you want to be his friend."

Heineman replies that the Goodrich management is confused about the sequence of events and seems to regard the use of a tender offer as a kind of antisocial act. "In expressing our interest through Lehman Brothers," says Heineman, "a respected investment-banking firm that had been engaged to find a merger partner for Goodrich, we believed that we were going to them directly. But, in any event, Goodrich has unparalleled arrogance in assuming that we first had to make an offer to management. We've gone to the *owners* of a business and said, 'we would like to make you an offer which you are free to accept or reject as you chose.' We haven't used coercion. We haven't bludgeoned anybody directly."

A GLACIAL SUMMIT IN AKRON

Despite the public rebuff by Keener, Heineman wanted to make one more effort to make a friendly deal with Goodrich. "It's not my style to raid anyone," he says. "We were still prepared to sit down and work out an arrangement." Three days after the announcement of his tender offer, Heineman, accompanied by Gaylord Freeman Jr., chairman and chief executive of the First National Bank of Chicago and a director of Northwest, journeyed to Akron to meet with Keener. The atmosphere was glacial. Keener sat behind his bare desk, along with Raphael Jeter, the chief counsel for Goodrich. To Keener's assertion that Heineman had not contacted him prior to the announcement, Heineman asked, "Didn't Lehman Brothers tell you?" After forty-five minutes it was clear to Heineman that Keener was determined to fight. "Mr. Keener had made up his mind that he didn't want any part of Northwest," says Heineman. "I thought him a very restricted man—that he'd been weaned too early as a baby." Keener says he cannot remember what he thought of Heineman.

In a letter sent to stockholders in February Keener said it had been hinted that he could become the chairman of the combined companies. "I rejected this approach out of hand," he wrote. "I could not place my own position ahead of your interests and those of over 47,000 employees, and neither would any other member of your management." Officers and directors of Northwest insist that no such offer was made.

Later Keener wrote to stockholders, "We want you to know that no member of the board and no corporate officer plans to exchange his shares and none of us has sold B. F. Goodrich shares since the offer was announced last January." The directors of Goodrich, however, owned only 55,465 shares among them, or .04 percent of the outstanding shares. Moreover, in the five-year period up to February 1, Keener, President Harry Warner, and Group Vice President William Perdriau had acquired little stock in their own company; they exercised the right to buy only 2,052 of the 45,700 shares granted under a stock-option plan.

For Heineman, the Goodrich take-over was intended to be the climax of three extraordinary careers. First, he was a successful lawyer. Then, in 1956, he was elected chairman of the Chicago & North Western Railway, a dying operation that became a big money spinner under Heineman's imaginative direction. (The North Western is probably the only road that makes money on its commuter hauls.) Heineman then set out to put together the largest railroad combination (in terms of mileage) in the nation. He acquired about 90 percent of the stock in the Milwaukee Road, and made an attempt to gain control of the Rock Island. The idea was to merge the three railroads into one midwestern system that would connect the powerful Penn Central in the East and Union Pacific in the West. Other railroads oppose the plan, which is pending before the ICC.

Heineman switched direction again in 1967, when he transformed his railroad into a holding company called Northwest Industries. The following year he negotiated a merger with Philadelphia & Reading Corp. (P. & R.), a successful conglomerate that had increased per-share earnings by an annual average rate of 11.22 percent in the decade up through 1967. P. & R. was a combination of medium-sized companies making consumer and industrial products that had been put together by Howard A. Newman from the dying embers of an old anthracite business. So high was Newman's reputation in banking circles that he had raised an $80-million credit line without collateral to buy Lone Star Steel. Now the biggest component of Northwest Industries, P. & R. accounted for 50 percent of its 1968 sales and 89 percent of its pretax profits excluding nonrecurring items.

With this merger, Heineman suddenly became an aggressive conglomerater. He made an attempt to acquire Home Insurance, but lost when City Investing topped his bid. However, he had the consolation of making a $16-million profit after taxes from the initial open-market purchases of Home Insurance stock. An attempt to merge with Swift came to nothing when Heineman decided that the value he had seen in the company was illusory. The stage was then set for another attempt at a major acquisition.

Heineman had his own reasons for moving fast. He had about made up his mind to wind up his career within two years, possibly to enter government service, or to write a book on the nation's transportation problems. Says Heineman, "You come to a point in your life when you ask yourself, 'What do you want to do? Do you just want to keep on making bigger companies out of littler ones?' " But before he left business, he wanted to turn Northwest into a major industrial entity, and the Northwest-Goodrich combination fitted his personal timetable nicely.

SOME NEW MATH AT WHITE & CASE

Shortly after the Northwest announcement, Keener assembled three law firms, two public-relations counselors, two investment-banking companies, and an accountant to advise him on the fine art of fending off Northwest. A lawyer's most effective defense against a take-over is to prevent the registration of securities offered in exchange for the stock of the target company. White & Case, Goodrich's regular attorneys, sought to accomplish this by asking various securities commissions to prohibit the registration of debentures and warrants offered by Northwest on the grounds that the offer was in violation of states' security laws.

But the White & Case analysis of Northwest's registration statement contained an extraordinary blunder. The law firm claimed that the company's existing debt-equity ratio was 75 to 1 and that the ratio would increase to more than 160 to 1 if the maximum $689 million in Northwest debentures was issued for the Goodrich stock. Apparently, White & Case arrived at these figures by dividing an inflated amount of Northwest debt by the number of shares outstanding instead of comparing the dollar amounts of debt and equity. Northwest's debt-equity ratio at the time was 40 percent to 60 percent equity, and even using the erroneous debt figure cited by White & Case the ratio, assuming complete acceptance of the exchange offer, would be 55 percent debt to 45 percent equity. Raphael Jeter, the Goodrich general counsel, claims that the letter was mailed without his knowledge. "I never saw it," he says. "We were so busy here in Akron that I didn't know whether we were walking or running." The White & Case attempt to bar registration of Northwest's securities failed in every state.

The difficulties that B. F. Goodrich faced in trying to make a defensive merger are spelled out in that January 31 memorandum that summed up the brainstorming sessions of the experts. The memorandum suggested that "the desirable growth rate of a company to be acquired should be based on the performance of Firestone, Goodyear, and Uniroyal and not BFG." A starkly candid analysis stated the problems that would arise if Goodrich acquired a number of small companies. "This will require," said the memo, "that we (1) view the footwear and industrial products industries as nongrowth industries, (2) withhold substantial capital expenditures for the tire company until it demonstrates that it can produce a satisfactory earnings growth, and (3) channel our cash flow into the new firms acquired." Seldom has a major corporation been so frank about its own weaknesses.

Of all the tactics devised by management to fend off Northwest, none was so extreme as the revision of Goodrich's bank-credit agreement. On February 3, thirteen days after Heineman announced his tender offer,

Goodrich increased its line of credit with twenty-one banks, headed by First National City, to $250 million, and at the same time amended the agreement so that the loan would be in default in the event of a take-over. Moreover, the company, according to the memorandum, was considering using up to $200 million of the loan to prepay such items as income taxes and accounts payable, and to make contributions to retirement funds. The intent was "to drive home to Mr. Heineman the fact that he will have to make arrangements to borrow this amount of money elsewhere in advance of the close of his tender offer."

The details of this extreme maneuver were revealed by the Goodrich lawyers during the final minutes of the Justice Department's antitrust case in Chicago last month. Judge Hubert L. Will was astonished. Likening the amendment to a "Herman Goering cyanide pill," Judge Will wondered why Goodrich would voluntarily enter into an agreement "under which it threatened to commit financial suicide in the event that this transaction is consummated. It's a shocking document. It's the worst indictment of Goodrich management of anything in the record in this case."

"WE ARE IN THE GRIP OF HYSTERIA"

The Northwest-Goodrich battle is a landmark in more ways than one. It was the Justice Department's first attempt to rejoin a would-be raider, and the first court hearing in its attempt to extend antitrust laws to include mergers and acquisitions that could result in concentration of manufacturing assets. (Antitrust cases involving I.T.T. and Automatic Canteen, and Ling-Temco-Vought and Jones & Laughlin, will not be heard until later this year.) After listening to the opening arguments, Judge Will said, "We are really faced with a whole new dimension of value judgments here."

To Ben Heineman, caught in the storm, the events of the past five months suggest a climate of management fear in many corporations. "At the moment," he says, "we are in the grip of an hysteria rising largely out of fear on the part of insecure and inadequate managements that's contrary to the best interests of stockholders. This fear may prevent shareowners from exercising appropriate control over the officers and directors who represent them. It may prevent them from realizing the true value of their securities. And I believe that there's going to be a time when many people will regret the extreme positions they are now taking, especially in stimulating the government to action."

But Ward Keener showed no signs of regret at all.

Questions

1. Evaluate Heineman's approach to Keener. Should he have been more "friendly," more blunt, more open, more secretive, or do you think he handled the approach as well as he could have?
2. Evaluate Goodrich's operating performance with the following question in mind: If you were a Goodrich stockholder, do you think the present management's performance has been sufficient to warrant your support in a proxy fight or tender offer?
3. If a management believes that a merger would not be in the best interests of its stockholders, then it should resist a merger offer. However, there are certainly limits beyond which management should not step in its resistance—some defensive actions would do irreparable harm to the company or its stockholders and should not be taken. Do you feel that B. F. Goodrich's defensive tactics, considered individually and as a group, are reasonable or unreasonable from this standpoint?
4. State what action you would take, and why you would take it, in each of the following situations: (a) You are a B. F. Goodrich stockholder asked to approve or disapprove of the proposed merger. You signify approval by tendering your stock. (b) You are a U.S. Congressman asked to vote in favor of legislation (unspecified here) that would be neutral in all respects except that it would aid Goodrich and similar companies to resist take-overs. (Assume, for purposes of this question, that existing antitrust laws are adequate to deal with the antitrust aspects of the case; that is, the proposed legislation is antiraider legislation, not antitrust legislation.)

Wilcox Chemicals, Inc.

(Multinational Business Finance)

Wilcox Chemicals, Inc., a major domestic producer of agricultural chemicals and fertilizers, is currently exploring possibilities for expanding its overseas operations. At present, its foreign operations consist primarily of exporting finished products, and in 1971 foreign sales represented only 5 percent of total sales. Warren Bradford, Vice President in charge of the International Division, feels that the company's foreign sales could be improved dramatically by establishing additional production facilities in foreign countries. Experience with a small plant in Asia has shown that local facilities improve sales by making it easier to design the product for specific needs and by facilitating technical assistance to customers. Also, if the plants are located properly, savings on transportation charges and labor can reduce the cost per unit of output.

In 1971, the International Division's Economic Planning Group began to evaluate a proposal for a plant in Caladan, a developing nation seeking to expand its agricultural industries. Although Caladan's agricultural techniques are not highly developed, its government has participated in several technical assistance programs with the United States and other countries, and Caladan appears to be on the verge of a marked long-term expansion. The Economic Planning Group concluded that Wilcox Chemicals could play an important role in this new market by establishing local facilities for research, production, and sales. Also, the experience and knowledge gained from participation in Caladanian development could be extremely valuable in any future attempts to establish operations in neighboring countries and in other parts of the world.

Estimates for the required investment in the proposed Wilcox-Caladan plant, to be constructed in 1972, are shown in Table 36.1. The uncertainty about the required investment outlay is due primarily to uncertainties regarding construction costs. Inflation and the shortage of skilled labor are the primary sources of concern. It is reasonably certain, however, that the plant could begin operations in 1973.

The estimated before-tax profits for a 20-year period are shown in Table 36.2. It is recognized that these estimates, especially those for the later years, are quite uncertain. As is explained below, Wilcox Chemical's own cash inflows from these earnings are subject to additional elements of uncertainty.

In addition to repatriated earnings of the Wilcox-Caladan operation, the parent firm would receive $100,000 per year (net of expenses and before taxes) in technical and supervisory fees. However, projected

Table 36.1

PROBABILITY DISTRIBUTION OF
WILCOX-CALADAN INVESTMENT REQUIREMENTS
(Millions of U.S. Dollars)

Cash Investment Required	Probability
$4.0	.1
4.5	.2
5.0	.4
6.0	.2
7.0	.1

Table 36.2

ESTIMATED EARNINGS OF WILCOX-CALADAN
(Millions of Caladan Pounds)

Year	Profit Before Tax	Caladanian Tax
1972	(£0.25)	£0.0
1973	0	0.0
1974	1.00	0.4
1975	1.50	0.6
1976–1981	2.00	0.8
1982–1991	1.75	0.7

profits of $200,000 per year (before tax) from current export sales to Caladan would be lost after the Caladanian plant begins operations in 1973.

The life of the project is somewhat uncertain. First, the expected economic life of the initial plant without any additional major investments should be approximately 10 years, although a life of 20 years is possible under favorable operating conditions. The productive capacity of the plant will be maintained, to some extent, by partial reinvestment of earnings, as required by Caladanian law. The major source of uncertainty, however, lies in the possibility that the government of Caladan may nationalize the plant. Nationalization of foreign firms has not occurred in the past, although the government of Caladan is strongly nationalistic and independent. The President of Caladan has given assurances that the hands-off policy will not be changed, and that in the unlikely event of nationalization, the firm will be given fair compensation for the plant. In spite of the obvious uncertainties involved, the Economic Planning Group has concluded that the present political situation in Caladan is conducive to foreign investment.

After consideration of the economic and political factors, the Economic Planning Group developed estimates for the life of the project and the conditional expected economic value of the plant at the end of each possible project life; these estimates are shown in Table 36.3. Although the estimates for the project life reflect, to the extent possible, the risk of expropriation of the plant by the Caladanian government, no attempt has been made to estimate the amount of compensation to be received if the plant is nationalized. Thus, the estimates for the terminal value of the plant reflect only the expected value of the plant under the assumption of no expropriation.

The Economic Planning Group's next task is to estimate the cash

Table 36.3

PROBABILITY DISTRIBUTIONS OF
PROJECT LIFE AND SALVAGE VALUE OF PLANT
(Millions of Caladan Pounds)

Probability of Project Life	Project Life[a]	Expected Value at End of Project Life
.1	3 years	£3.0
.2	6	3.0
.5	10	2.5
.1	15	1.5
.1	20	1.0

[a] The project life includes the construction year, 1972.

inflows to the parent firm. These inflows will include repatriated earnings, which are limited by Caladanian law to 80 percent of net profits after Caladanian taxes (but before U.S. taxes), plus the $100,000 fee income. Also, the inflows must show a negative entry to account for the lost export sales. Since income from other Wilcox subsidiaries is consolidated with domestic operations, the analysts assume that the same practice will apply to Wilcox-Caladan. The full earnings (before Caladanian taxes) of Wilcox-Caladan will be subject to U.S. taxes at the rate of 50 percent. In addition, Wilcox-Caladan earnings are subject to local Caladanian taxes at the rate of 40 percent, although the U.S. tax liability is reduced by the amount of local taxes paid. Thus, the net U.S. tax liability is 10 percent of the before-tax earnings of Wilcox-Caladan, although the effective tax rate on repatriated earnings is, of course, somewhat higher. The dollar value of the repatriated earnings will depend on the exchange rate.

At the time of the study, the official exchange rate was $2.50 to one Caladan pound.[1] The Caladanian Central Bank is attempting to stabilize the rate at this level pending the expected realignment in international currency exchanges. However, due to the inflationary pressures on the pound, there is a good chance that the exchange rate will fall considerably. The magnitude of change is uncertain and will depend largely on the Caladanian government's ability to control inflation. Under current estimates, the exchange rate will fall to around $2.25 to one pound in 1973, then stabilize at around $2.00 to one pound in 1974. This downward shift in the exchange rate will result in a reduction in the dollar value of repatriated earnings and, in addition, the book value of Wilcox-Caladan will be reduced by approximately $300,000 in 1973 and 1974.

Although initial plans specify the establishment of Wilcox-Caladan as a wholly-owned subsidiary of Wilcox Chemicals, Inc., a joint venture with Caladanian investors is a distinct possibility. The source of debt financing is another unresolved issue. Initial plans call for 50 percent equity financing, with about one-half of that amount in the form of equipment. The 50 percent debt financing could be obtained from several sources. The Central Bank of Caladan has indicated a willingness to lend the equivalent of $1 million at an interest rate of 12 percent; no parent company guarantee would be involved in this loan. Wilcox-Caladan could also obtain up to $1 million from U.S. banks at an interest rate of approximately 8 percent; a parent company guarantee would be required. In addition, funds could be raised in the Eurodollar or Eurobond markets at 8½ and 9 percent, respectively, again with the obligation guaranteed by the parent firm.

---

[1] The pound is the Caladanian unit of exchange.

Because of the several alternative sources of capital, each with a different cost, there has been considerable debate over the appropriate cost of capital for this project. Wilcox Chemical's average cost of capital for U.S. investments is 10 percent, but projects range from a low of 8 percent to a high of 14 percent. One of Mr. Bradford's assistants has suggested that cash flows should be discounted at 14 percent, the required rate of return for high-risk projects in the United States. Another staff member has argued that an even higher cost of capital should be used because the project is overseas. A third analyst has suggested that the cost of capital cannot be determined until the method of financing has been decided upon. Mr. Bradford himself is uncertain about the appropriate cost of capital, and, in addition, wonders about the possibility of using a *lower* than average cost of capital for this project because of possible portfolio effects (the world economy and the U.S. economy may, over the next 10-20 years, move in somewhat divergent directions).

Questions

1. Compute the net present value of the project to Wilcox Chemicals, Inc., at the beginning of 1972. Assume: (a) the plant is established as a wholly-owned subsidiary; (b) Wilcox-Caladan income is consolidated with parent firm income; and (c) the discount rate is 14 percent. Note the following conditions on taxes and repatriated earnings: (a) The 50 percent U.S. tax rate is applied to the total earnings of the subsidiary *before* local taxes; (b) Wilcox is given a U.S. tax credit in the amount of Caladanian taxes paid; (c) Repatriated earnings (before U.S. taxes) are 80 percent of the net profit of Wilcox-Caladan after local taxes but before U.S. taxes; (d) Ignore the devaluation loss in the book value of the assets of the subsidiary in your tax and cash flow calculations. (HINT: Calculate the expected project life, find the corresponding terminal value of the plant at the end of the project life (an expected-value calculation is not needed to find the terminal value once the project life is determined), and then compute the NPV based on that project life and terminal plant value. This calculating sequence is easier than alternative sequences.)

2. How would the NPV of the project be affected if Wilcox Chemicals elected to receive its returns from the Caladanian plant in the form of dividends rather than consolidating the Caladanian income with domestic income? (Give only the probable direction of the change.) Under what condition would Wilcox Chemicals prefer to consolidate income from subsidiaries rather than receive dividends? Does this situation appear to exist in the present case?

3. Evaluate the choice of a wholly-owned subsidiary versus a joint venture with Caladanian investors.

4. Design and justify an appropriate financing mix for the project (the 50-50 debt-equity mix need not be used). Be sure to indicate the effects of the following factors, among others, on the financing program: (a) relative rates of inflation in the U.S. and Caladan, (b) quotas on U.S. direct investments, and (c) the chance of expropriation.

5. What cost of capital do you feel is appropriate for this project? Why?

6. What effect would the devaluation of the assets of Wilcox-Caladan have on (a) the parent firm's consolidated earnings, (b) cash flows?

7. Should Wilcox Chemicals go ahead with the project?

Idaho Potato Packers, Inc.

(Voluntary Reorganization)

When Thomas Marlborough, founder of Idaho Potato Packers, Inc., died in March 1970, his position as president and chairman of the board of the company was assumed by his nephew, William Remington. Although Idaho Potato had experienced severe difficulties in recent years, Remington believed that the problems could be overcome by the infusion of some new capital. The company's liquidity position was weak, and much of its equipment was in need of replacement. Because of its poor liquidity position, relatively low current earnings, and history of losses in recent years, Idaho Potato could not arrange additional debt financing. Investment bankers had, however, informed Remington that it would be possible to float a new issue of common stock, but only on the condition that preferred dividend arrearages were eliminated. As long as the preferred stock was in arrears, no dividends could be paid on the common stock, and the investment bankers felt that a new issue of common stock could not be sold as long as common dividends were restricted.

Idaho Potato was founded in 1934 as a potato distribution company. Thomas Marlborough experimented with dried mashed potatoes, and during World War II he obtained sizable contracts from both the army and navy to supply dehydrated potatoes to the armed forces. After the war, the company continued with its dehydrated potato operations, and it also expanded into frozen stuffed-baked and French-fried potatoes.

The company prospered during this period, and by 1960 it was one of the largest producers and marketers of frozen potato products.

In the early 1960s, the market for frozen potatoes seemed unlimited, so Idaho Potato and other producers expanded to meet the market demand, doubling the industry capacity between 1961 and 1963. Market demand did increase over the two-year period, but not as fast as the industry expanded its productive capacity. The result was inevitable. Prices were slashed, but firms still operated at far less than full capacity. All firms in the industry were suffering losses, and a number of companies were forced into bankruptcy. Idaho Potato came very close to suffering this fate in 1965, when a $2.5 million bond issue matured, but the company managed to obtain cash to retire the bonds by the sale of certain of its distribution facilities.

Idaho Potato's 1961–1963 expansion was financed in part by the sale of a $2.5 million issue of 6 percent preferred stock to five insurance companies and in part by retained earnings. Dividends were paid on the preferred stock in 1962, 1963, and 1964, but no dividends have been paid on the preferred since 1964. By the end of 1970, preferred dividend arrearages totaled $900,000, and until these arrearages are paid, no cash dividends may be paid on the common stock. Some statistics on the company are given in Tables 37.1 and 37.2.

Industry sales and profits improved after 1967, but Idaho Potato's physical plant and financial position were both in relatively bad shape. Although a new physical plant was added in the 1961–1963 expansion, it had not been well maintained, and new processing-equipment developments had made much of Idaho's equipment obsolete. William Remington believes, however, that approximately $1.5 million of new funds would put the company back into a strong competitive position.

Table 37.1

IDAHO POTATO PACKERS, INC.
SUMMARY OF SALES AND PROFITS, 1963–1969

Year	Sales (in thousands)	Profits[a] (in thousands)	Price Range of Stock
1963	$3,777.5	$352.5	$156–128
1964	3,117.5	137.5	96–65
1965	2,437.5	(37.5)	67–11
1966	1,862.5	(227.5)	12–4½
1967	1,525.0	(267.5)	5–2¼
1968	1,730.0	25	11–4½
1969	1,885.0	45	21½–7¼

[a] Excludes write-offs and losses on sale of assets totaling $3,163 million.

Table   37.2

IDAHO POTATO PACKERS, INC.
YEAR ENDED DECEMBER 31
(in thousands)

	1963	1967	1969
Assets			
Cash	$ 462.5	$ 265.0	$ 325.0
Accounts receivable	1,055.0	347.5	742.5
Inventories	1,767.5	610.0	717.5
Total current assets	$ 3,285.0	$1,222.5	$1,785.0
Total fixed assets	7,447.5	2,845.0	2,605.0
Total assets	$10,732.5	$4,067.5	$4,390.0
Liabilities			
Accounts payable	$1,220.0	$ 770.0	$ 674.5
Accruals	400.0	355.0	683.0
Other current liabilities	260.0	147.5	167.5
Total current liabilities	$ 1,880.0	$1,272.5	$1,525.0
Bonds	$ 2,500.0	—	—
Preferred stock ($100 par)	2,500.0	$2,500.0	$2,500.0
Common stock ($100 par)	1,250.0	1,250.0	1,250.0
Surplus	2,602.5	955.0d	885.0d
Total long-term liabilities	$ 8,852.5	$2,795.0	$2,865.0
Total liabilities	$10,732.5	$4,067.5	$4,390.0

Idaho Potato's common stock is currently selling at about $27 a share in the over the counter market. The preferred stock is not publicly traded, so no market price has been established for it. The investment bankers have indicated that they would purchase, for resale to the public, 60,000 shares of common stock to net the company $25 a share—if the preferred stock arrearages are eliminated. Remington has scheduled a meeting with the attorney representing the five insurance companies which hold Idaho Potato's preferred stock, and he hopes to work out a recapitalization plan to eliminate the arrearages.

Questions

1. Assume that the preferred stockholders are willing to turn in their preferred shares and receive common stock in exchange for both the preferred stock and the dividend arrearages. How many shares of common stock should be given for each of preferred? Give both a lower limit, or minimum amount that preferred stockhold-

ers should accept, and an upper limit, or maximum amount that Remington should offer, as well as what you consider to be the most reasonable figure. Justify your reasoning for each of these figures.

2. Given the facts of this case, what exchange ratio do you think would actually be used? Give consideration to the relative bargaining positions of the two parties.

Part VII

Integrated View of Financial Management

Case /38

Jensen Motors
(Timing of Financial Policy)

Jensen Motors, a large manufacturer of engines used in lawn-mowers, boats, power tools, and the like, was almost acquired by Gulf & Eastern Industries, a major conglomerate, in 1969. Jensen management resisted the merger, and, with the aid of the Davenport Foundation, a non-profit organization established by Horace Davenport, founder of Jensen Motors, the take-over bid was successfully warded off. However, the foundation's trustees indicated some dissatisfaction with Jensen Motors' performance during the past few years. They noted that, although sales have been expanding rapidly, earnings, dividends, and the price of the company's stock have not been keeping pace. Jensen Motors' management, in return for the foundation's aid in resisting the take-over, agreed to undergo a thorough review of present management practices and policies and then to make whatever changes seem necessary for improving the firm's performance.

To aid in making the review, Jensen Motors retained the management consulting firm of McKinley & Company, one aspect of whose survey is an appraisal of the policy decisions in the major functional areas, including the financial area. For purposes of the study, McKinley has divided the finance function into two parts: (1) internal operations, encompassing the effectiveness of financial controls over the various divisions, capital budgeting, and credit policy, and (2) external financing policies, comprised principally of the methods used in obtaining funds and the timing of financial policy. Roger Brinkley, the McKinley & Company partner who is directing the Jensen Motors study, is well aware of the sensitive nature of his report, particularly the effect it will have on the career of Thomas Rentz, Vice President, Finance. If Brinkley's report is favorable, Rentz will be given a substantial salary increase and additional corporate responsibilities. If, on the other hand, the report is unfavorable, Rentz's progress will be arrested. In fact, given the pressures now on the company, there is even a possibility that Rentz will be fired.

Brinkley notes that Rentz has an accounting background, having been brought into Jensen Motors from the accounting firm of Pierce-Waterford in 1955 as controller. Rentz was elevated to Vice President, Finance, in 1957. Brinkley is also aware that Rentz attended an executive development program at Northwestern University during the academic year 1963–1964. Rentz finished at the top of his class at Northwestern, and his performance in the area of corporate finance was especially meritorious.

Brinkley's analysis indicates that Jensen Motors' internal financial operations are outstanding. The company has a well-organized system of financial controls, and its capital budgeting procedures are as modern as any that Brinkley has ever encountered. Brinkley has not completed his appraisal of Jensen Motors' external financing policies, but he has assembled the following information on the company's past financing arrangements.

1958 FINANCING

In early 1958, Jensen Motors required a substantial amount of new external funds. From 1954 through 1957 sales had grown at a rate of about 5 percent a year, but earnings had been relatively constant, held down because (1) research and development expenditures were very high during this period and (2) new plant facilities had been required to produce the products generated by the research and development program, and the start-up cost of these new facilities had not yet been offset by increased revenues.

The price of the stock in 1958 was approximately $10 a share, while the earnings per share were $1. Other firms in the industry were selling at price-earnings ratios of about 18, but the rest of the industry had been showing significantly better growth trends in earnings per share. Jensen Motors' debt ratio in 1958 was 24 percent versus 38 percent for the industry.

The company needed to increase total assets from $70 million to $91 million, or by approximately 30 percent. Since $6 million of these funds would be obtained from earnings retained during 1958, approximately $15 million of new external funds would be required. The first alternative open to the company was a one-year bank loan at a current interest rate of 4.04 percent. The company would be able to renew this loan at the end of one year at the then going interest rate, provided the firm's financial position was still sound. A second alternative was long-term, non-convertible bonds yielding 4½ percent, while the third option was to sell common stock to net the company $9 a share. On the recommendation of Rentz, Jensen Motors sold $10 million worth of common stock and obtained $5 million in the form of a short-term bank loan.

1960 FINANCING

The additional productive facilities opened in 1958 enabled Jensen Motors to take advantage of the new products developed earlier under the research and development program. Earnings increased from $1 to $4 a share, and the price of the stock rose from $10 to $88. In 1960, although the investment community regarded Jensen Motors as a growth company because of its recent earnings growth, the management of Jensen Motors believed that this label was probably inaccurate. Since increased competition from other companies was cutting into profit margins, and because no new products were in sight in the research and development department, management expected growth to slow down to about 5 percent a year, more in line with the national growth rate.

Jensen Motors needed no additional outside funds to finance its operations in 1960, but the company did need to finance a merger acquisition. The owner of Woodward Products Company, a manufacturer of motor housing units and a major supplier to Jensen Motors, wanted to sell his company and retire. Jensen Motors decided that the acquisition should be undertaken. In the past, the firm had experienced difficulty at certain times in receiving a steady supply of high-quality motor housings, and Jensen felt that, if it acquired Woodward Products, this problem could be alleviated.

The agreed-upon price for Woodward Products was $15 million. Mr. Woodward was willing either to sell out for cash or to accept stock of Jensen Motors with a value of $15 million. Rentz recommended the cash purchase, and this method of acquisition was agreed to by the Jensen Motors board of directors. Since Jensen Motors had no excess cash at the time, the $15 million was borrowed from a life insurance company on a five-year, 5 percent note. Short-term bank loans were, at the time, available at a 5½ percent rate of interest.

1965 REFUNDING

Anticipating inflationary pressure as a result of the increased intensity of the Vietnam war, Rentz expected a rising level of interest rates in 1965. Accordingly, he decided that it would be a good idea to refund Jensen Motors' short-term debt, which had risen to $25 million by 1965. On Rentz's recommendation, Jensen Motors directors authorized the issuance of $25 million of 5.2 percent, 25-year bonds and then used the proceeds to retire $25 million of short-term bank loans carrying a current interest rate of 5 percent.

1968 FINANCING

Jensen Motors' steady, if not spectacular, growth required additional financing in 1968. The stock had been split three for one in 1963, and in 1968, it was selling for $35 and earning $2.20 a share. The industry average price-earnings ratio at the time was 16. A policy of retaining most of its earnings had enabled Jensen Motors to reduce its debt ratio from 47 percent in 1965 to 36 percent, which closely approximated the industry average of 37 percent, by 1968.

Jensen Motors' total assets, in 1968, were $148 million. The company needed $15 million over and above the amount that would be generated by retained earnings to finance its continued growth. The required funds could have been obtained by using short-term debt at an interest rate of 7½ percent, long-term nonconvertible debt at the same rate of interest, convertibles carrying an interest rate of 6½ percent that would be convertible into common stock at $40 a share, or common stock that would be sold to net the company $33 a share. On Rentz's recommendation, convertibles were used to obtain the $15 million.

Questions

1. Evaluate Rentz's financing decisions made in each of the following years: (a) 1958, (b) 1960, (c) 1965, and (d) 1968.
2. Do his decisions seem to be improving over time?
3. How should Roger Brinkley evaluate Thomas Rentz's overall performance, and what recommendation as to his future should he make? Give *adequate consideration* to both internal financial operations and external financing operations.

Murray, Finch, Price, Farmer & Smith

(Suggested Financing Alternatives)

To obtain a position in the underwriting department of a major investment banking house is difficult, but it is especially hard to land a job that calls for contact with the top partners so that one may learn the inside of the business. Through family connections, however, Gordon Hammrick was fortunate enough to get the job of assistant to William Murray, Senior Partner and Managing Officer of Murray, Finch, Price, Farmer & Smith. Hammrick received his bachelor's degree in history only two weeks ago, and this is his first day on the job. After a rather pleasant morning spent meeting various people around the office, including some attractive secretaries, Hammrick was given his first task.

Murray had not only been forced to miss his regular Thursday afternoon golf match, but he also had to stay up until 3 A.M. Thursday night finishing some recommendations on the types of financing that a group of clients should use. The next morning, having completed the analyses and made his recommendations, Murray turned over to Hammrick the folder on each client and, attached to each of the folders, the recommendations as to the types of financing that each should use. He then told Hammrick, first, to have the analyses and financing recommendations typed up and sent immediately to each of the client companies and, second, that he was taking his secretary away for a weekend of uninterrupted dictation. Murray particularly stressed that he should be contacted during the weekend only in the event of an emergency.

The first thing Hammrick did was to detach the analyses and recommendations from the folders and give them to one of the secretaries to type up. When the secretary returned the typed reports, Hammrick discovered that he did not know which recommendation belonged to which company! He had folders on nine different companies and financing recommendations for nine companies, but he could not match them up. Hammrick's major was history, so he could not be expected to be able to match the financing recommendations with the appropriate companies. However, as a finance student, you should be able to help Hammrick by telling him which companies in Section B should use the financing methods shown in Section A.

SECTION A

1. Common stock: nonrights.
2. Debt with warrants.
3. Factoring.
4. Friends or relatives.
5. Preferred stock (nonconvertible).
6. Common stock: rights offering.
7. Long-term bonds.
8. Leasing arrangement.
9. Convertible debentures.

SECTION B

(a) Arizona Mining Company

Arizona Mining needs $10 million to finance the acquisition of mineral rights to some land in south-central Arizona, as well as to pay for some extensive surveys, core-borings, magnetic aerial surveys, and other types of analyses designed to determine whether the mineral deposits on this land warrant development. If the tests are favorable, the company will need an additional $10 million. Arizona Mining's common stock is currently selling at $12, while the company is earning approximately $1 a share. Other firms in the industry sell at from 10 to 15 times earnings. Arizona Mining's debt ratio is 25 percent, which compares with an industry average of 30 percent. Total assets at the last balance sheet date were $105 million.

(b) New York Power Company

Since New York Power, a major electric utility, is organized as a holding company, the Security and Exchange Commission must approve all security issues; such approval is automatic if the company stays within conventional norms for the public utility industry. Reasonable norms call for long-term debt in the range of 55–65 percent, preferred stock in the range of 0–15 percent, and common equity in the range of 25–35 percent. New York Power Company currently has total assets of $1 billion financed as follows: $600 million debt, $50 million preferred stock, and $350 million common equity. The company plans to raise an additional $25 million at this time.

(c) Wilson Brothers, Inc.

A wholesale grocery business in Cincinnati, Ohio, this company is incorporated with each of the three Wilson brothers owning one third of the outstanding stock. The company is profitable, but rapid growth has put it under a severe financial strain. The real estate is all under mortgage to an insurance company, the inventory is being used under a blanket chattel mortgage to secure a bank line of credit, and the accounts receivable are being factored. With total assets of $5 million, the company now needs an additional $100,000 to purchase 20 forklift trucks and related equipment to facilitate handling in the shipping and receiving department.

(d) Alabama Milling Company

Alabama Milling manufactures unbleached cotton cloth, then bleaches the cloth and dyes it in various colors and patterns. The finished cloth is packaged in bulk and sold on 60-day credit terms, largely to relatively small clothing companies operating in the New York City area. The company's plant and equipment have been financed in part by a mortgage loan, and this is the only long-term debt. Raw materials— cotton and dyes—are purchased on terms calling for payment within 30 days of receipt of goods, but no discounts are offered. Because the national economy is currently so prosperous, apparel sales have experienced a sharp increase. This, in turn, has produced a marked increase in the demand for Alabama Milling's products. To finance a higher level of output, Alabama Milling needs approximately $500,000.

(e) Florida-Pacific Corporation

Florida-Pacific is a major producer of plywood, paper, and other forest products. The company's stock is widely held, actively traded, and listed on the New York Stock Exchange; recently it has been trading in the range of $30–$35 a share. The latest 12 months' earnings were $2.12; the current dividend rate is 80 cents a year, and earnings, dividends, and the price of the company's stock have been growing at a rate of about 7 percent over the last few years. Florida-Pacific's debt ratio is currently 42 percent versus 25 percent for other large forest product firms. Other firms in the industry, on the average, have been growing at a rate of about 5 percent a year, and their stocks have been selling at a price earnings ratio of about 13. Florida-Pacific has an opportunity to acquire a substantial stand of forest in Northern California. The current owners of the property are asking $20 million in cash for the land and timber.

(f) Toy World

Joseph Marino is an employee of the state of Pennsylvania and an avid model airplane and model automobile builder, and he has just learned that some of the stores in a new neighborhood shopping center are still available to be leased. Marino knows that no good toy and hobby store exists in the southwest section of the city of Harrisburg, and he believes that if he can obtain approximately $20,000 for fixtures and stock, he can open a successful store in the new shopping center. His liquid savings total $5,000, so Marino needs an additional $15,000 to open the proposed store.

(g) Knight Electronics Corporation

Knight Electronics is a medium-sized electronics company whose sales distribution is approximately 30 percent for defense contracts and 70 percent for nonmilitary uses. The company has been growing rapidly in recent years, and projections based on current research and development prospects call for continued growth at a rate of 10–12 percent a year. Although recent reports of several brokerage firms suggest that the firm's rate of growth might be slowing down, Knight's management believes, on the basis of internal information, that no decline is in sight. The company's stock, which is traded on the Pacific Stock Exchange, is selling at 20 times earnings; this is slightly below the 23 times ratio of Standard & Poor's electronics industry average. The firm's debt ratio is 40 percent, just above the 38 percent average for the industry. The company has assets of $28 million and needs an additional $4 million, over and above retained earnings, to support the projected level of growth during the next 12 months.

(h) Utah Chemical Company

Utah Chemical is a closely held company that was founded in 1952 to extract minerals used in agricultural fertilizers from the Great Salt Lake. The company's debt ratio is 48 percent versus an average ratio of 36 percent for agricultural fertilizer producers in general. The stock is owned in equal parts by 10 individuals, none of whom is in a position to put additional funds into the business. Sales for the most recent year were $10 million, and earnings after taxes amounted to $600,000. Total assets, as of the latest balance sheet, were $8 million. Utah Chemical needs an additional $3 million to finance expansion during the current fiscal year, and, given the worldwide growth in demand for agricultural chemicals, the firm can anticipate additional outside capital needs in the years ahead.

(i) Universal Container Corporation

Universal Container is engaged in the manufacture of cans, glass bottles, paper boxes of various sorts, a variety of plastic tubes, and other packaging materials. Since the firm sells to a great many producers of nondurable consumer goods, sales are relatively stable. The current price of the company's stock, which is listed on the New York Stock Exchange, is $42, and the most recent earnings and dividends per share are $4 and $2, respectively. The rate of growth in sales, earnings, and dividends in the last few years has averaged 5 percent. Universal Container has total assets of $360 million. Current liabilities, which consist primarily of accounts payable and accruals, are $25 million; long-term debt is $75 million; and common equity totals $260 million. An additional $30 million of external funds is required to build and equip a new can-manufacturing complex in central California and to supply the new facility with working capital.

PRESENT VALUE OF $1

Year	1%	2%	3%	4%	5%	6%	7%	8%	9%	10%	12%	14%	15%
1	.990	.980	.971	.962	.952	.943	.935	.926	.917	.909	.893	.877	.870
2	.980	.961	.943	.925	.907	.890	.873	.857	.842	.826	.797	.769	.756
3	.971	.942	.915	.889	.864	.840	.816	.794	.772	.751	.712	.675	.658
4	.961	.924	.889	.855	.823	.792	.763	.735	.708	.683	.636	.592	.572
5	.951	.906	.863	.822	.784	.747	.713	.681	.650	.621	.567	.519	.497
6	.942	.888	.838	.790	.746	.705	.666	.630	.596	.564	.507	.456	.432
7	.933	.871	.813	.760	.711	.665	.623	.583	.547	.513	.452	.400	.376
8	.923	.853	.789	.731	.677	.627	.582	.540	.502	.467	.404	.351	.327
9	.914	.837	.766	.703	.645	.592	.544	.500	.460	.424	.361	.308	.284
10	.905	.820	.744	.676	.614	.558	.508	.463	.422	.386	.322	.270	.247
11	.896	.804	.722	.650	.585	.527	.475	.429	.388	.350	.287	.237	.215
12	.887	.788	.701	.625	.557	.497	.444	.397	.356	.319	.257	.208	.187
13	.879	.773	.681	.601	.530	.469	.415	.368	.326	.290	.229	.182	.163
14	.870	.758	.661	.577	.505	.442	.388	.340	.299	.263	.205	.160	.141
15	.861	.743	.642	.555	.481	.417	.362	.315	.275	.239	.183	.140	.123
16	.853	.728	.623	.534	.458	.394	.339	.292	.252	.218	.163	.123	.107
17	.844	.714	.605	.513	.436	.371	.317	.270	.231	.198	.146	.108	.093
18	.836	.700	.587	.494	.416	.350	.296	.250	.212	.180	.130	.095	.081
19	.828	.686	.570	.475	.396	.331	.276	.232	.194	.164	.116	.083	.070
20	.820	.673	.554	.456	.377	.312	.258	.215	.178	.149	.104	.073	.061
25	.780	.610	.478	.375	.295	.233	.184	.146	.116	.092	.059	.038	.030
30	.742	.552	.412	.308	.231	.174	.131	.099	.075	.057	.033	.020	.015

Year	16%	18%	20%	24%	28%	32%	36%	40%	50%	60%	70%	80%	90%
1	.862	.847	.833	.806	.781	.758	.735	.714	.667	.625	.588	.556	.526
2	.743	.718	.694	.650	.610	.574	.541	.510	.444	.391	.346	.309	.277
3	.641	.609	.579	.524	.477	.435	.398	.364	.296	.244	.204	.171	.146
4	.552	.516	.482	.423	.373	.329	.292	.260	.198	.153	.120	.095	.077
5	.476	.437	.402	.341	.291	.250	.215	.186	.132	.095	.070	.053	.040
6	.410	.370	.335	.275	.227	.189	.158	.133	.088	.060	.041	.029	.021
7	.354	.314	.279	.222	.178	.143	.116	.095	.059	.037	.024	.016	.011
8	.305	.266	.233	.179	.139	.108	.085	.068	.039	.023	.014	.009	.006
9	.263	.226	.194	.144	.108	.082	.063	.048	.026	.015	.008	.005	.003
10	.227	.191	.162	.116	.085	.062	.046	.035	.017	.009	.005	.003	.002
11	.195	.162	.135	.094	.066	.047	.034	.025	.012	.006	.003	.002	.001
12	.168	.137	.112	.076	.052	.036	.025	.018	.008	.004	.002	.001	.001
13	.145	.116	.093	.061	.040	.027	.018	.013	.005	.002	.001	.001	.000
14	.125	.099	.078	.049	.032	.021	.014	.009	.003	.001	.001	.000	.000
15	.108	.084	.065	.040	.025	.016	.010	.006	.002	.001	.000	.000	.000
16	.093	.071	.054	.032	.019	.012	.007	.005	.002	.001	.000	.000	
17	.080	.080	.045	.026	.015	.009	.005	.003	.001	.000	.000		
18	.089	.051	.038	.021	.012	.007	.004	.002	.001	.000	.000		
19	.030	.043	.031	.017	.009	.005	.003	.002	.000	.000			
20	.051	.037	.026	.014	.007	.004	.002	.001	.000	.000			
25	.024	.016	.010	.005	.002	.001	.000	.000					
30	.012	.007	.004	.002	.001	.000	.000						

PRESENT VALUE OF AN ANNUITY OF $1

Year	1%	2%	3%	4%	5%	6%	7%	8%	9%	10%
1	0.990	0.980	0.971	0.962	0.952	0.943	0.935	0.926	0.917	0.909
2	1.970	1.942	1.913	1.886	1.859	1.833	1.808	1.783	1.759	1.736
3	2.941	2.884	2.829	2.775	2.723	2.673	2.624	2.577	2.531	2.487
4	3.902	3.808	3.717	3.630	3.546	3.465	3.387	3.312	3.240	3.170
5	4.853	4.713	4.580	4.452	4.329	4.212	4.100	3.993	3.890	3.791
6	5.795	5.601	5.417	5.242	5.076	4.917	4.766	4.623	4.486	4.355
7	6.728	6.472	6.230	6.002	5.786	5.582	5.389	5.206	5.033	4.868
8	7.652	7.325	7.020	6.733	6.463	6.210	5.971	5.747	5.535	5.335
9	8.566	8.162	7.786	7.435	7.108	6.802	6.515	6.247	5.985	5.759
10	9.471	8.983	8.530	8.111	7.722	7.360	7.024	6.710	6.418	6.145
11	10.368	9.787	9.253	8.760	8.306	7.887	7.499	7.139	6.805	6.495
12	11.255	10.575	9.954	9.385	8.863	8.384	7.943	7.536	7.161	6.814
13	12.134	11.348	10.635	9.986	9.394	8.853	8.358	7.904	7.487	7.103
14	13.004	12.106	11.296	10.563	9.899	9.295	8.745	8.244	7.786	7.367
15	13.865	12.849	11.938	11.118	10.380	9.712	9.108	8.559	8.060	7.606
16	14.718	13.578	12.561	11.652	10.838	10.106	9.447	8.851	8.312	7.824
17	15.562	14.292	13.166	12.166	11.274	10.477	9.763	9.122	8.544	8.022
18	16.398	14.992	13.754	12.659	11.690	10.828	10.059	9.372	8.756	8.201
19	17.226	15.678	14.324	13.134	12.085	11.158	10.336	9.604	8.950	8.365
20	18.046	16.351	14.877	13.590	12.462	11.470	10.594	9.818	9.128	8.514
25	22.023	19.523	17.413	15.622	14.094	12.783	11.654	10.675	9.823	9.077
30	25.808	22.397	19.600	17.292	15.373	13.765	12.409	11.258	10.274	9.427

Year	12%	14%	16%	18%	20%	24%	28%	32%	36%
1	0.893	0.877	0.862	0.847	0.833	0.806	0.781	0.758	0.735
2	1.690	1.647	1.605	1.566	1.528	1.457	1.392	1.332	1.276
3	2.402	2.322	2.246	2.174	2.106	1.981	1.868	1.766	1.674
4	3.037	2.914	2.798	2.690	2.589	2.404	2.241	2.096	1.966
5	3.605	3.433	3.274	3.127	2.991	2.745	2.532	2.345	2.181
6	4.111	3.889	3.685	3.498	3.326	3.020	2.759	2.534	2.339
7	4.564	4.288	4.039	3.812	3.605	3.242	2.937	2.678	2.455
8	4.968	4.639	4.344	4.078	3.837	3.421	3.076	2.786	2.540
9	5.328	4.946	4.607	4.303	4.031	3.566	3.184	2.868	2.603
10	5.650	5.216	4.833	4.494	4.193	3.682	3.269	2.930	2.650
11	5.988	5.453	5.029	4.656	4.327	3.776	3.335	2.978	2.683
12	6.194	5.660	5.197	4.793	4.439	3.851	3.387	3.013	2.708
13	6.424	5.842	5.342	4.910	4.533	3.912	3.427	3.040	2.727
14	6.628	6.002	5.468	5.008	4.611	3.962	3.459	3.061	2.740
15	6.811	6.142	5.575	5.092	4.675	4.001	3.483	3.076	2.750
16	6.974	6.265	5.669	5.162	4.730	4.033	3.503	3.088	2.758
17	7.120	5.373	5.749	4.222	4.775	4.059	3.518	3.097	2.763
18	7.250	6.467	5.818	5.273	4.812	4.080	3.529	3.104	2.767
19	7.366	6.550	5.877	5.316	4.844	4.097	3.539	3.109	2.770
20	7.469	6.623	5.929	5.353	4.870	4.110	3.546	3.113	2.772
25	7.843	6.873	6.097	5.467	4.948	4.147	3.564	3.122	2.776
30	8.055	7.003	6.177	5.517	4.979	4.160	3.569	3.124	2.778